Through the Eyes of a Seer

Kelly J Caselman

Through the Eyes of a Seer
One Man's Testimony of Seeing into the Supernatural

By
Kelly Caselman

ISBN: 978-1-7336960-0-5

DEDICATION

To my wonderful family, I couldn't have done this without you,
To my wife, Kara, and my children, Alexandra, Mikayla, Logan.

Contents

Acknowledgments 6

Introduction 7

1 Flashback to my Childhood 19

2 Keeping My Focus 44

3 Back Home with Mom 71

4 Demonic Manifestation 99

5 Shots Fired 117

6 Basic Military Training (BMT) 149

7 Touring History in Europe 195

8 Home—Some Things Never Change 266

9 Coming Full Circle 279

Kelly J Caselman

ACKNOWLEDGMENTS

A special thank you to everyone who contributed to the completion of this book. To my wife, Kara, for her patience and editing, Virginia McCreey for her time and editing, Cole Henry for his graphic design that brought the bookcover to life and Alexandra Caselman for her artwork.

Introduction

Throughout the Old Testament, as well as the New Testament, the Bible speaks of seers and prophets. Nathan, Elijah, Samuel, Elisha, and Jeremiah were a few of the men mentioned in the Bible to have this gift. But most of us ask, Is the ability to see into the spirit realm by way of our natural eyes, our mind's eye, or visions and dreams? When did this first start for these great men of God? Did they have the spiritual gift from birth, or did it come upon them later in their life and their walk with God? If they did have this ability as a child, what were their struggles? Were there other men and women who had this gift but never opened their mouths due to fear of ridicule and persecution because they did not have the faith that these men possessed? Were some of these people thrown into prison for insanity or put into insane asylums to try to help them, or, in our modern day, medicated to the point of uselessness to try to conform them so they would fit into normal society?

In the New Testament, Paul, Stephen, and John also had dreams, visions, and the ability to see. Paul was the man who wrote much of the New Testament; what if he and these other great men had given in and allowed themselves to be silenced by society? These questions are hard to answer, but the scriptures speak of many spiritual gifts, such as mercy, leadership, giving, exhortation, teaching, and serving. The list goes on and mentions the gift of prophecy, or, as the Old Testament calls it, a seer. As for myself, I have come to terms with the fact that I am a seer, but I will never be called a prophet. I see what God allows me to see, and it has taken me most of my life to understand what it is that I do. The larger question for me was, Why me? But then you must ask yourself, Why can some people sing, and why are other people blessed with the gift of speaking? These are also gifts from God that are hard for the individual to explain.

Does a seer see all the time? Does a person who is gifted to sing, sing all the time? Does an individual who is a gifted speaker continually speak? No. They sing when God calls them to sing, they speak when God tells them to speak, and a seer can see when God allows him or her to see.

Question: What is a seer in the Bible? Answer: a seer is a person who sees by supernatural insight. In the Bible, a seer is another name for prophet. "In those days, if people wanted a message from God, they would say, 'Let's go and ask the seer,' for prophets used to be called seers" (1 Samuel 9:9 New Living Translation).

God spoke to his people through prophets in different ways, and one way was through visions accompanied by the ability to interpret what God was saying by these visions. We see different verses throughout the Bible speaking about Seers or prophets:

As they were climbing the hill to the town, they met some young women coming out to draw water. So Saul and his servant asked, "Is the seer here today?" (1 Samuel 9:11 NLT)

The next morning the word of the Lord came to the prophet Gad, who was David's seer." (2 Samuel 24:11 NLT)

The rest of the events of Solomon's reign, from beginning to end, are recorded in The Record of Nathan the Prophet, and The Prophecy of Ahijah from Shiloh, and also in The Visions of Iddo the Seer, concerning Jeroboam son of Nebat. (2 Chronicles 9:29 NLT).

Then the Lord said to me, "Look, Jeremiah! What do you see?" And I replied, "I see a branch from an almond tree."

And the Lord said, "That's right, and it means that I am watching, and I will certainly carry out all my plans." Then the Lord spoke to me again and asked, "What do you see now?"

And I replied, "I see a pot of boiling water spilling from the north."
"Yes," the Lord said, "For terror from the north will boil out on the people of this land. Listen! I am calling the armies of the kingdoms of the north to come to Jerusalem. I, the LORD, have spoken." (Jeremiah 1:11–18 NLT)

But Stephen, full of the Holy Spirit, gazed steadily into heaven and saw the glory of God, and he saw Jesus standing in the place of honor at God's right hand. And he told them, "Look, I see the heavens opened and the Son of Man standing in the place of honor at God's right hand!" (Acts 7:55–56 NLT)

It was the Lord's Day, and I was worshiping in the Spirit. Suddenly, I heard behind me a loud voice like a trumpet blast. It said, "Write in a book everything you see, and send it to the seven churches in the cities of Ephesus, Smyrna, Pergamum, Thyatira, Sardis, Philadelphia, and Laodicea."
When I turned to see who was speaking to me, I saw seven gold lampstands. And standing in the middle of the lampstands was someone like the Son of Man. He was wearing a long robe with a gold sash across his chest. His head and his hair were white like wool, as white

as snow. And his eyes were like flames of fire. His feet were like polished bronze refined in a furnace, and his voice thundered like mighty ocean waves. He held seven stars in his right hand, and a sharp two-edged sword came from his mouth. And his face was like the sun in all its brilliance.

When I saw him, I fell at his feet as if I were dead. But he laid his right hand on me and said, "Don't be afraid! I am the First and the Last. I am the living one. I died, but look—I am alive forever and ever! And I hold the keys of death and the grave.

"Write down what you have seen—both the things that are now happening and the things that will happen." (Revelations 1:10–19 NLT)

Chapter 1

I have laid down a base of biblical truths that seers do exist, and I would like to take you on my journey as I found out for myself what it is like to be a modern-day seer. And so my story begins. As we drove through the hills into a heavily wooded area of the Black Forest in Germany, we came to a parking area where many cars were parked. I asked my friend, "So where are you taking me now?"

She said, "Remember when I told you I wanted you to meet some people I know?"

Looking at all the cars I thought, "Wherever we are going, there must be a lot of people."

She smiled at me and said, "Most of these people are here to go to a viewing area of the Black Forest, but we're not going there."

I thought, "Of course not. Why would we?"

So we got out of her car and started to walk on a small path into the forest. We were both in pretty good shape, since we were in this country by way of the US military. Although she was in administrations, she was an avid long-distance runner, and I was a maintenance troop who had been cross-trained into security forces / special operations. I hoped I had been trained well enough to handle what I was about to get into.

My friend and I had both been blessed with the ability to see in the spirit, so you could call us "seers." After walking for about fifteen minutes, I stopped and asked, "Just exactly where are we going?"

All she would say was "You'll see."

I told her I didn't really like surprises. When my team jumped out of airplanes, we had a pretty good idea of where we were going and what was going to happen when we arrived. So I reminded her that I didn't like surprises, and she said, "You worry too much. These people are like us. They see in the spirit."

I asked, "Do they see like you and play with demonic spirits, or do they see like me and cast them out in Jesus's name?"

I'm sure that most people would have stopped and gone back to the car, but part of me was curious, and the other part of me thought I was bulletproof. Either way, I was intrigued to find out what was on the other end of this path.

Soon after that, in the distance, I could see a chain-link fence with barbed wire along the top. It had a German sign on it. In large red letters it read, WARNUNG FERNHALTEN. Translated, that means Warning Keep Out.

I looked at my friend and asked, "I guess that sign's not talking about us, right?"

We kept walking along the fence line until we arrived at a point where it looked as if someone had taken a hacksaw and cut the bottom off one of the posts. There was also a symbol etched onto the post that I was unfamiliar with. She told me to pull up on one side of the post. As I did, I noticed that the posts on either side of this one had been cut as well, so this made it easy to pull up on the fence. She slid underneath while I held the post. Once she was in, she held the post for me and I slid under as well. As I stood up, I still didn't see anything but more forest.

Again we kept walking until we got to a large mound. At that point, I could see what looked like a cellar door with steps leading down to it. There was a large padlock on the door, and as it had been with the fence posts, someone was very handy with a hacksaw. Even though it appeared to be locked, the door was easy to open. With a loud creaking noise coming from the door, we walked down another set of stairs. As we moved farther down into what seemed to be an old fallout shelter, the smell was very musty, and I could see a dim light coming from the bottom of the stairs. As we went farther inside, I started to hear people talking. Out of habit from when I was a kid, a verse from Psalm 23 popped into my mind. Under my breath, I spoke the words that I knew so well. As I spoke the verse, a sense of peace came over me. For some reason God had brought me to this point, right here, right now.

My friend took my hand at the bottom of the stairs, and we walked down the hallway. There were doors on both sides, and in each doorway, there was a large candle about the size of a coffee can. We stopped just before going into an open door, and she asked me if I was OK with this. I told her that she had obviously brought me this far for a reason, and I was curious to find out why. At that, we walked into a room that was much larger than I thought it was going to be. In this abandoned underground shelter, there were at least fifty metal-framed bunk beds along one wall, most with rotted mattresses. Very large metal tables sat in the middle of the room. There were some chairs, but most were broken, or the seats were missing. The graffiti on the walls was lit by what appeared to be about a hundred candles, the only illumination in the room. On the table, there were small animal bones and a circle of candles with knives next to them. On a different table, there were several rotting birds. Some of the men in the room stood up as we walked in. My friend, still holding my hand, stood silent as one of the men said, "Oh, how sweet. You brought your boyfriend."

He was the boldest one in the room, because he walked up to me and asked if I was scared.

I asked, "Why? Should I be?"

He turned around and walked away, muttering, "Because most people are."

In my mind I went from Psalm 23 to Psalm 91. I wasn't about to let fear manifest its ugly head at this point. Another guy stood up and walked toward us as if he was trying to size me up. He walked around us, and as he made a circle, he grabbed the chicken bones off the table, spit on them, and threw them at my feet. At this point, my friend abruptly let go of my hand and walked over to where the other women were in the room. As I stood there alone now, I couldn't decide what was worse—the smell of body odor or the stench of dead poultry on the table. Even though there were so many candles, the darkness in the room was almost as thick as the concentration camp where my friend and I had first met.

In the spirit, demonic entities far outnumbered the people in the room, and some appeared to have demons protruding from their bodies. This was something I was unfamiliar with, and I now know it to be demonic possession. Most of the other people in the room had two or three entities huddled around them. I motioned to my friend to come back to where I was still standing, but I could see two demonic entities that had come next to her as well. The guy who had circled around my friend and me picked up a knife and began to flip it into the air and catch it. At times it landed in his hand blade first, so blood was dripping from his fingers. At that, one of the girls went over to him and licked the blood off his hand.

I looked at my friend and said in a loud voice, "So why am I here?"

The man who had walked up to me at the beginning said, "I understand you can see in the spirit, and in this room, that's not unique. We can all see in the spirit." He added, "I have also been told that you don't like playing with demonic entities. Do you have any idea in the world what they can allow you to do?"

As he said this, one of the knives flew off the table into his hand, by way of a demonic spirit. He looked at me and asked, "Will your God allow you to do that?"

He said something in German, and another guy put his hand under one of the large tables. As he did this, I could see many demonic entities under the same table, and they lifted it. In the natural, it looked as if the young man was lifting the table with one hand, but in truth, it was the demonic entities that he was entertaining. He motioned to a girl in the room and directed her in German to stand in front of me about eight feet away. I watched as several demons put their hands on her and lifted her off the ground about three feet into the air. The man looked at me and smiled.

I said, "This would all be entertaining if I couldn't see in the spirit, but I can. The prophets of Baal were able to perform the same tricks, but if I remember right, the prophet Elijah was not amused."

The man with the knife in his hand slammed the blade down into the dead animal on the table. Two of the other men stood up and said, "Do we really need to put up with this guy?"

They turned and looked at the girl who had brought me and asked, "Why did you bring him here?"

The girl next to her grabbed my friend by the hair and held her still. With that, the three men looked at me and said, "You know that very few people are aware of this place. And we get the feeling that you have a very big mouth."

At that moment the demonic entities began moving around the room, crawling up and down the three men. Other entities moved about the room and put out half of the candles that were lit, to make the room darker. My mind played out each step of how this fight was going to go. As I stood there, in the spirit, I knew it would never get to that point because Psalms 91:7 says, "A thousand shall fall at thy side, and ten thousand at thy right hand, but it shall not come upon thee." This fight was of the Lord! God started to show me things, almost as if my life was flashing before me. I saw myself as a child when I first began to see in the spirit. In all the struggles that I had been through, God had been preparing me for this moment so that I would not move away from his light or fall into the darkness that was all around me. My preparation had started many years ago. The days that had seemed meaningless in my past became very relevant, and in what was a matter of seconds, my entire life began to play out before my eyes.

Flashback to My Childhood

I was born in Southern California in December 1960. Many things come to mind of this time and place, including hippies, drugs, free love, and rock music. My family, for being Californian in the early sixties was, as I thought, a "normal family." I was the youngest of four, and I had three older sisters. My dad was a construction worker who had served in the navy during World War II, and as far as I remember, my mom didn't work outside the home. We lived in a middle-class neighborhood, and I didn't think much about the direction my life was going. I was just a child, but I knew things were different for me. In the beginning, my family just assumed I had an overactive imagination, and like a lot of kids, I had an imaginary friend, which seemed pretty normal for a four- or five-year-old. For whatever reason, the things I saw were different, and from a young age, the "imaginary friends" that I thought were obvious to everyone were, in reality, only obvious to me.

My neighborhood friends, classmates, and I would play Little League football and Little League baseball; most of the time, my dad was our coach. I was athletically inclined, but my studies were a lot more complicated, and my seeing in the spirit was very distracting in school. It wasn't as if the classroom was full of demonic activity; more like here and there and not always every day, but it was a break from being in my home environment where it was a never-ending circus.

When entering kindergarten in the early sixties, we were all given a choice of a dog tag or a bracelet. I was a little boy, and a bracelet was just a little too girly for me, so like all the other boys, I received a type of dog tag. On it was your name, phone number, address, and parents' names. On the other side you could have engraved pretty much anything you wanted. I really didn't know what I wanted, so my teacher, God bless her, decided for me that I would have a verse from Psalm 23: "The Lord is my shepherd, I shall not want, he leads me in paths of righteousness."

It was around that time I began to understand that I could see things. I was a shy kid, and I never really heard anyone else talk about these things. I wasn't sure whether it was a good thing or a bad thing. I just knew it was a thing. I had the ability to see things, and they dismissed it as my imagination, my imaginary friends, and at one point my family would make fun of me and say things like "Oh, are your imaginary friends here?" Little did they know my imaginary friends really weren't with me. They were actually following my family.

***

I grew up in a household that did not go to church. My dad would say things such as "Good bread, good meat, good God, let's eat." And that was our family prayer. They spent a lot of time drinking alcohol, smoking pot, and doing an assortment of other drugs. Every person in my family smoked cigarettes. Sometimes, to be funny, they would roll up all the windows in the car, give me a straw, and let me breathe air through it with the window barely cracked open. There was also a lot of physical contact in my household, most of which took place with very little clothing on. As a young kid, I witnessed these activities and saw what was going on around the people who were participating, so I stayed quiet because what I saw, nobody else seemed to notice.

But unfortunately, I did. Many times I asked my friends, "Do you see anything right there with that guy?" Or "Do you see somebody standing next to my sister?"

They would just look at me funny and say, "No, your sister is *fine*."

I urged them more and said, "No, not my sister. Do you see anything around my sister?"

They had no idea what I was talking about, and I couldn't put it into words because I didn't know how to describe it. I continued to ask other friends, and they just thought I was a bit strange. Once when I was six years old, I asked my mom, "You can see me and you can see Dad and you can see my sisters, but do you see anyone else?"

She said, "Yes, I can see you."

I told her that was not what I meant and asked her again if she could see the other people.

She asked, "Other people?"

"Yes," I said. "They're not really little, but they're smaller than we are."

She said, "I don't know what you're talking about, son. Are they your imaginary friends?"

I didn't want to talk about it, so I discontinued the conversation. She obviously did not see what was going on around my family members.

***

Around this same time, these figures started coming up to me as well, sometimes as close as three or four inches from my face. I'd seen them for so long that it didn't seem like a big deal, but I didn't want them in my personal space. When I went to bed, I would pull the covers all the way over my head because they would come in my room and get close to my face and just stare at me. I didn't like that, so I would pull the sheet up, leaving only enough space for my eyes to peek out. It was so uncomfortable to sleep like that because it was hot, but for some reason, I told myself that my covers would protect me, like a blanket of protection. I didn't know why, but I just felt safer with the blankets over me.

The entities weren't always there, but they would usually appear when my family was home. As a kid, I spent a lot of time by myself at the house. That was nice because the "imaginary friends" weren't there, but when my family came home, within a short period of time, I would see the entities reenter the house.

The entities looked about the size of chimpanzees, with the hair singed off. They had patches of hair here and there, and they were always slightly deformed. They looked as if they were in pain and were grimacing as if they'd been hurt and couldn't heal. They also had an odd smell. Looking back, I realize that I learned to identify their presence based on a particular smell.

I always thought it was strange when I went to school; they were hardly ever there. I saw more of a white light with my teacher, but it was just light and not much of a figure. However, I always felt safe with her, something I didn't always feel at home.

School was a nice change from the darkness of my house. At home, I always knew there would be cigarette smoke and that funny-smelling smoke that had become such a part of my home. My dad would come home from work and start drinking a six-pack of beer. He would say things to me such as "Here, take a drink of this. It'll put hair on your chest." It never did, and it tasted awful. Luckily, while he was drinking beer, we would usually play catch with the football or baseball. There's one thing I can say about my dad. He may have drunk quite a bit of beer, but he was probably my best friend when I was a kid.

Once when I was in my room, I could hear my mom and dad fighting. It always scared me when they fought, so I peeked out the door, and the little hairless chimpanzees were moving around them in a stir. There were several of them in the room. Even though the door was closed, they would come into my room. It didn't matter to them that the door was shut. They didn't have a need to open the door. They just walked through the wall. That was always strange to me, but it was all I ever knew, so it seemed normal. I remember sitting on my bed as they stared at me and came close to my face, looking at me. I don't know why, but I reached down and grabbed the dog tag that my kindergarten teacher had given me. I looked at this little hairless entity that was in my face and said the words that were printed on the back of my name tag. "The Lord is my shepherd, I shall not want. He leads me in paths of righteousness" (Psalms 23:1–3 KJV).

Immediately I looked up, and the little entities moved back five or six feet and just looked at me in terror. They couldn't comprehend why I had said those words, and in truth, I didn't know why I had said them either. I found out that day, sitting on my bed, that the words on the back of this necklace would make these entities move away from me, and that was a good thing. I tested my theory when I walked into the house and saw these little figures. Under my breath, I would just say, "The Lord is my shepherd, I shall not want. He leads me in paths of righteousness." And it got their attention.

They would all look at me, back away, and, as I walked, move out of the way. It was the greatest revelation. I had no understanding of how I had stumbled upon something that seemed to work, but when I spoke the words from Psalm 23, it was as if there was a force field around me, and it made a profound difference in how they responded to me.

I didn't know it at the time, but I would come to understand that this verse would actually shape the rest of my life. The Bible says that there is power in our words. Therefore, what I said was "The Lord is my shepherd." I know that doesn't sound like much, but what I was doing was professing over my life that the Lord *is* my shepherd—not he *was* my shepherd, not that he *will be* my shepherd, but that he *is* my shepherd.

The next words I said were "I shall not want." Again, I was professing over my life—that I will want for nothing. My Lord will provide all my needs, all my wants, all my desires. I shall not want for anything. He is my Jehovah Jireh, my provider.

Next, I spoke, "He leads me in the paths of righteousness." In other words, he was keeping me on a righteous path—to seek him, to know him, to trust in him. He would be my El Shaddai.

All these things would become real to me later in life, but for now I was just a little boy who needed to feel secure.

My family and friends would notice me looking at something and ask, "What are you looking at? You just seem to be staring off into space."

It's something I never really got used to, because as the creatures moved around the room, they would catch my eye. I would spot them from my peripheral vision, and the natural reaction was to turn my head. We had a dog and two cats, and I figured out when I was still quite small that they sometimes turned their heads or would be staring off at what seemed to be nothing. Somehow I knew they saw what I saw: the entities moving in the room. At times I felt I had more in common with the animals of our household than I did with my family.

Trying to Understand My Gift

Our house was small, probably no more than 1,000 square feet, with two bedrooms and one bathroom, but the yard seemed huge. I spent the majority of my time outside, like most kids of that era, but it also kept me away from what was going on inside the walls of our house. When I was seven or eight, we moved to a different house that was larger, around 1,500 square feet, with four bedrooms and two bathrooms. It seemed like a castle to me. Since I was the only boy in the family, I had my own room; my youngest sister and my middle sister shared a room, and my older sister had her own room.

This was the house that I would spend most of my childhood in, and an abundance of my memories would stem from this house. For some reason, I thought that having my own room would mean I wouldn't have to deal with little entities running around the house, but I was wrong. They seemed to come and go as they pleased, but because of my newfound scripture, it was easier to keep them at bay. It was at this house that they would talk to me for the first time, but I was never afraid of them. It was like growing up with a family pet that had always been there.

As I mentioned before, arguments seemed to excite the entities. I saw them whisper in my family members' ears. I didn't know what they said, but seeing the outcome led me to realize the escalation of what they were capable of causing.

Since my father was in construction and would be gone sometimes for days or weeks or more, my sisters, my mom, and I would remain at the house. I don't recall seeing my mother very often. I don't know where she was. My sisters would bring friends over, and these entities seemed to multiply. Some of them would point at me and whisper to one another. They somehow knew that I could see them and would move back and forth in the room and watch my eyes follow them. Then they would go speak to others, and they would do the same, moving back and forth in the room and watching my eyes. They would sometimes come and talk to me. This was the first time I heard them say "seer," but since I was so young and didn't know anything about the Bible, I thought they were saying "sear," like you would sear a steak before eating it.

When I was around the age of eight or nine, my family bought a Ouija board. Ironically enough, it was a Christmas gift for one of my sisters. When their friends would come over, they would get the Ouija board out, and the entities would stir. I didn't know it was because of the Ouija board.

One time they asked me if I wanted to play with them. The entities looked at me in surprise, and one of them said, "Go ahead. See what happens."

So I put my hands over the piece that is supposed to move across the board, and at that moment, one the entities put his hand under the piece that is supposed to move across the board and lifted it off the board about two inches. My sisters and their friends stared in amazement because they didn't understand what was happening. I wasn't really sure myself, but the entity moved the Ouija piece to different letters on the board. As the window lined up over letters on the board, it spelled out the word "seer."

One of my sister's friends asked, "What does that mean?"

It wasn't as if they could Google it, but I knew what it meant, and I kept quiet. My sister's friends asked me if I could do other things. As it turned out, these entities would move forks toward me on the table, cause small items to levitate under my hand, and bend spoons like wax. These things were done to the amazement of my sisters and their friends, who were sometimes under the influence of marijuana or alcohol. I believe the words they used were "Far out, man."

It seemed that among my sister's friends, I was somewhat of a novelty, but I was still not able to tell them what was truly going on. As I paid more attention, I realized that these entities could tell me what was going on, and from what I saw, my family gave in to these entities' suggestions very easily, sometimes with no resistance at all. Now, when I think back, I may have been able to foresee more than I realized. I knew when my parents were going to have fights because of how the entities would move about them and whisper. My parents would give in to the words that were spoken to them as if the entities had some form of control over them. My family was an easy target, since alcohol, pot, and free love seemed to be in abundance in my neck of the woods.

***

I remember playing Little League baseball. As a pitcher, I noticed that if I threw the ball close to the batter, one of these entities would show up. I would later realize that the entity had something to do with "fear," and the person, when I would throw a curveball, would stand there in fear and strike out, sometimes just flailing at the ball. Other times, these batters would walk up to the plate, and the entities were already there. The batter would already be afraid, fearful, as if to say, please don't hit me with that ball.

I was pretty good at putting the ball where I wanted, but I knew when any of these guys came to the plate, he was probably so afraid that he would strike out, make himself look silly, or get hit by the ball. I would wonder if other kids could see the same fear following these children around. As the kids would strike out and go back to the dugout, the entity would stay with them and tell them how terrible they were, making them doubt themselves. They would sit on the bench and sometimes cry. The coach would yell at them while most of the players made fun of them.

I was said to be a very good pitcher, but the truth was that I learned to recognize that fear could be physically seen, and when I saw fear with them, I would exploit it. From time to time, I would ask a teammate if he could see that little chimpanzee-looking thing over there with that kid. The teammate would look at me and shake his head, wrinkle his nose, and say something like "You're a good pitcher, but you're kind of weird." That was just more incentive for me to stay quiet, because I had finally found something I was good at, and because I was shy by nature, I kept my secrets well.

Wanting to Be Heard

When I was about nine or ten, we went to my dad's company picnic. I don't remember a lot about the picnic other than the fact that they broke up into teams and were playing a softball game. There was a light rain, and a friend, his dad, and I found a place under a large tree to watch the game. My friend sat with his back against the tree, seated on the ground. His dad stood to one side with his arm outstretched and one hand on the tree. I was standing maybe two feet from the tree, just watching the game, trying to stay dry. I heard a loud crack, and then everything went crazy. I was thrown face down on the ground, my ears were ringing, and the backs of my legs and the back side of my torso felt as if I had an extreme sunburn. I smelled burnt hair or something like it, but I didn't realize what had happened. Later I would find out that lightning had hit the tree. My friend, who had been seated on the ground with his back to the tree, had died. His father, who was standing with his arm outstretched with his hand on the tree, lost his arm from the elbow down. I was the lucky one who was thrown a short distance from the tree. As I lay there, I knew I couldn't get up.

My mom came to help the injured people, and when she got to me, she froze. The clothes on my back were partially disintegrated, and I had first- or second-degree burns on my back. I was dizzy. I looked to one side, and my neck hurt. I saw a white light, some type of a figure, and I asked my mom, "What is that white light? It looks like a person."

She said I probably had a concussion and was just imagining things. When more people gathered around, I could see entities that caused fear, and they seemed to be running rampant. I recall seeing the white figure take my friend by the hand. It wasn't so scary at that point. It just seemed like a calm peace. I watched them as they ascended. I could not get up to see very well, and I lost sight of them. I had so many questions and absolutely no answers. Obviously, after the lightning strike happened, they stopped the company picnic, and the injured, including me, were transported to the hospital.

***

After the lightning strike, I wanted to talk to my mom because I had questions about the white lights I had seen my friend go with. I also wanted to ask about the other figures that I had been seeing for so long. I wanted to tell her that I could see things, so quietly I asked, "Mom, why do I see these things and no one else does?"

She just looked at me. She must have thought it was the result of a concussion, and I don't remember her giving me any answer. After about four to five weeks, a concussion was no longer an excuse, and she asked me if my imaginary friends were still there.

I said, "Yes, they're always there."

She said, "I'm worried about you, and I want you to talk to someone."

I thought, "Great! Someone I can talk to about this. Maybe they can see them too."

So an appointment was made, and I had high hopes. The day came, and I went to see a psychiatrist. He asked me questions, and in the beginning of the interview, I opened up and was honest with him, but it did not take me long to figure out that he did not believe me. He seemed to think that either I was making all this up in my head or that there were things wrong with me that I needed medication to fix. I didn't understand why it was a bad thing that I saw the images that I saw, especially when I was playing baseball, because it made me better, but the doctor convinced my parents that he knew best.

Medication was prescribed. I had no idea what to expect. All I knew was I was just a kid. I really tried to do what I was told, so I took the medication. My parents thought it was a good idea, and I don't believe my sisters even knew that I had gone to see the psychiatrist.

The day after we had seen the doctor, my mom gave me my pill for the first time. It made me feel dopey and slow. Luckily, it was on a Saturday, and I didn't have school, because I'm not sure that I could've done anything on that first day. On the second day, it was just as bad, though I could still see the entities, so it didn't change that. By this time there was no way in the world I was ever going to say anything again.

By Monday, I had realized that I couldn't function with these pills, so when my mom gave one to me, I just went around the corner. Luckily, the bathroom was right next to my room. I would get up to use the bathroom, drop the pill in the toilet, and flush. After the initial prescription ran out, I told my mom what I was doing, because we didn't have much money. I knew I would get in trouble. And I did, because flushing this medication down the toilet was a waste of perfectly good cigarette and alcohol money.

***

Being shy had lots of benefits. I learned that I could say very little, but I could pay attention more than anybody knew. There were so many more things for me to watch, and it began to distract me in school because I would see things out of my peripheral vision. I would turn my head, and the teacher would say, "What are you looking at? There's nothing there."

I thought, "Right, there's nothing there. I knew that." But still it would distract me from my work, and about the best I could do was a C average. The teachers would tell my parents that I was easily distracted and they couldn't keep me focused. In today's schoolroom, they would call that some type of attention deficit, but if you could see what I saw, it would be hard to focus.

I continued to do mediocre work in school, but I excelled in sports because I understood how to use people's fear as an asset to me. It seemed the more I understood about what I was able to do, the more I could use it to manipulate situations with my parents, my sisters, and even my classmates, but most of all, situations while playing sports. I had learned to cheat in my own way.

***

Sometime around age ten, I started to play football because my dad wanted me to. He was a football fan as well as a baseball fan, but football was his first love; baseball was mine. I knew how to use my gifts to my benefit me in baseball, but in football I would have to do things a little differently.

I'm not positive, but I think the entity of fear came upon most of the players on the football field, including me. Luckily, I could run fast and catch a football. The coaches made me a receiver, which was a good thing because when other kids got scared, they were yelled at and told to go back in the game, but when I ran out of fear, they would just say, "Boy, that kid can run. Hope he can catch too."

In Little League football, the quarterback was a friend of mine, as well as the center, who was his brother. We practiced all the time together, and it made for a very good combination. My friend would hike the ball to his brother, who would then throw the ball to me. And with fear guiding me, I would run as fast as I could. Football was OK, catching the ball was fun, scoring touchdowns was even better, and as always, winning was the best.

Back in school, I was moved to the classrooms where the special-education kids went. I never understood it because they were different from me and looked different, and everyone made fun of us. Even the kids in the class would ask me, "Why are you here?" And my friends would say, "Are you going to stay in class with the special-education kids?" I didn't know what to tell them. I wished I could be back in the classroom with the rest of my friends. I guessed I would just have to learn to control the things I was seeing a little better, but at ten years old, that was easier said than done.

Back at home, things continued to get worse. The fighting and the drugs seemed to be escalating, and so was the population of these small entities that seemed to congregate in and around my house. I could keep them at bay. I had the dog tag around my neck that helped with that. "The Lord is my shepherd, I shall not want, he leads me in paths of righteousness," I would say, not knowing that it was a Bible scripture, just knowing that somehow these words had power. As chaotic and crowded as my household had become, uttering these words under my breath would create a bubble around me as I walked through what I know now was the valley of the shadow of death.

I was still a party favorite with my sisters and their friends, and more than once they asked me if I could do any tricks. I thought, "Heck, I don't even know how I do the ones that I do."

With that, these entities taught me a new trick. Two of them would put their hands under my feet and allow me to levitate about three to six inches off the ground as my sisters' and their friends' mouths would gape open. They would say things like "Man, you're freaking me out."

I was never amazed, because I knew how this was happening. I wasn't doing anything on my own, but I was the only one who knew, so I went along with it.

Chapter 2

It was about this time that my life would start to change in a drastic way. My parents had been driving somewhere, and all I knew was there was a car wreck. I was ten years old at the time, so it was around 1970. The car was totaled. In those days, seatbelts were not mandatory, and my parents went to the hospital. My two younger sisters and I went to live with some friends of the family; they were good people and treated us like grandkids. I don't know how long we stayed there, but I do remember that my mom had to have some type of back surgery, and my dad must've had some internal injuries.

Mom was released from the hospital first, but we weren't able to go home because she needed time to get back on her feet. Eventually we did go back home, and my mom seemed to be OK, but I noticed that she started drinking more. She didn't drink beer, but she would drink wine, and she smoked about four packs of cigarettes a day. The doctor told her that for rehabilitation to strengthen her back, swimming was a good idea, so my mom went down to the local YMCA and started to swim. About that same time, my dad was released from the hospital and had staples from about his belt all the way up to his chest, or, as he would say, "From stern to starboard."

He would walk around the house very gingerly and needed help sitting down and getting up. At that time my older sister had come back to the house. One evening my dad, my mom, and my older sister got into a huge fight. The entities were stirred and were moving about. They would whisper in their ears, almost like a puppeteer making his puppet dance. It escalated and ended with my oldest sister kicking my dad in the stomach and ripping the staples. I thought he would die. They took him to the hospital and had to do some type of surgery on him again.

My oldest sister stayed in the house that night. I remember sitting in my room, and one of these entities came in as if to console me. This time, I didn't use my magic verse. I just sat and listened to the words that it spoke to me, and it made sense. My dad had a shotgun in his bedroom. I was angry, and the small, hairless entity knew that. It seemed to prey upon my anger. I went into my father's room while my mom was asleep, and I took the double-barreled shotgun out from under the bed. I knew how it worked because I had used it many times. I checked to make sure it was loaded, and then I went to my big sister's room and opened her door. I leveled the gun at her. I don't know if one of my other sisters saw me, or if it was my mom, but I do remember a voice saying, "You don't want to do this."

About that time, my older sister woke up and saw me standing there about twelve feet away, and she started to cry. I just stood my ground, not sure exactly what I wanted to do, but I knew I wanted to create pain in her. I knew I wanted to hurt her like she had hurt my dad, but the words from my mom and my sisters were still behind me, saying, "You don't want to do this; please don't do this. We've had enough happen today."

The standoff seemed to last for an hour, but it was probably more like minutes. I pointed the shotgun toward the floor, handed it to my mom, turned, walked to my room, and closed the door behind me. Multiple entities came into the room with me and chattered something that sounded like "Go back and finish it. You're not done. Why didn't you do it? Are you a coward?"

Honestly, I'm not sure why I didn't do it. Probably because I didn't want to make my mom cry. My oldest sister left after that and married a guy who was in the army, and I don't remember her coming back to the house very often.

When my dad returned home, things went back to the way they had been before, minus my older sister. My middle sister also married and moved out during that time, and my mom started going to the YMCA every day. She had a whole new group of friends, something she hadn't had before, and at the Y, she was the life of the party.

Her swimming got so strong that she became a swimming instructor at the YMCA. Later, she began teaching handicapped kids how to swim. In the summer she would have me come and help out for a summer job. I would clean the locker room, help kids get to the pool, collect towels—all tasks that I didn't need much experience to do. The thing that I remember the most was in the office where the adults were. There were male and female instructors, and when they thought I was with the kids, or not looking, they would grab one another in places they shouldn't have.

After all the lessons were done for the day, they would break out bottles of wine and start drinking. I had to stay around and clean up the locker rooms and watch while their party started early. When I was done, I would get on my bicycle and ride home. My mom would stay there until they decided to move the party to someone's house. Sometimes, guys would bring my mom home that evening or the next morning, usually with a headache. The entities that were around them were significantly different, and they even looked different from the ones I was used to seeing. And by now I had identified several different entities. One would seem to make people do things of a sexual nature, another wanted to deceive people, pain and sickness seemed to be attached to a different one, and fear was still the one I saw the most. I was starting to notice patterns.

My dad seemed to have his own agenda by this time, and my parents spent less and less time together. My dad was not innocent; he was just more discrete. My mom didn't hide things from anyone, but by the entities I saw with my dad, I knew there was something going on. Something was in the works, and it was not good.

Keeping My Focus

Baseball continued, and I got better and better at it. Fear seemed to be a tool that I could use and be recognized at what I did. I was asked less and less to do my little performances at my sisters' parties. It seemed I had no control over when I was able to do these things and was only able to do them when the entities allowed me to. But in baseball, I didn't need anyone to show me how to manipulate the system. I used the entity of fear on my behalf and would make the all-stars when I was eleven and twelve. An umpire once came to me after a game where I had struck out sixteen batters, caught one pop fly, fielded a grounder, and threw out the person on first base. He brought a baseball to me and asked if I would sign it, stating, "Someday this baseball will be worth something."

It was about then that my mom and dad dropped a bomb on us—well at least me, because I was the only kid living at home. My sisters had all married, divorced, and married again. My parents were getting a divorce. To a twelve-year-old kid, that was about the worst thing that could happen. What I didn't know was that the path they had been on, for years, had been leading to this inevitable end.

I was to stay with my dad, which at the time I thought was fine. I didn't really know where my mom went, and I didn't see her very often, if ever. Now that it was just my dad and me in the house, the entities slowed down some, but they still followed him around, talking with him in quiet, low tones. I knew something was happening, but I just didn't know what.

Then my dad announced to me that he and his first wife were getting back together, and she was coming to live with us. I really didn't know what this meant. My relationship with my mom wasn't that good, and now there was going to be a new person. It seemed that my dad had been planning this well before he and my mom were divorced. My dad and his first wife had talked quite a bit on the phone, and I guess she was coming out to see if they could rekindle an old flame. When she arrived, multiple entities came with her, and they caused fear in me. I didn't like feeling the fear, because when I looked over my shoulder, I saw the entity of fear with me as well.

This new person in my dad's life would talk very nice to me in front of people, but the minute it was just her and me, it would get bad very quickly. I always knew it was coming because the entities would start talking to her, surrounding and swirling about her. Being alone with her would always invoke fear in me, a fear I didn't know with my biological mother, father, or sisters. It was a fear that this person was capable of doing things, was not to be trusted, could do physical damage to me, and the only thing I could possibly do was run. For the first time, this entity that I had been seeing for most of my life was following me. He would say things to me such as "Seer, can you see me?" It would only come to me when I was alone with her. When my sisters or my dad was in the room, it wasn't there, and she acted all happy. But when people weren't looking, she would look at me with eyes that I knew I couldn't trust. Before long, this person was living at my house, and the time of my dad and me being alone together was over. Everything in my life had changed, and more was about to follow.

***

My dad told me that I was to go live with my sister for the summer. My youngest sister had also married a man who was in the army and stationed in Kansas. She and I had gotten along well, and my brother-in-law was always good to me, so when it came time to go to my sister's house, it sounded like fun. However, during this time, my dad remarried his first wife, sold our house, and moved everything into a small apartment, this all happening with me not knowing anything.

While I was in Kansas, I saw parts of the country I hadn't known existed and met people who thought I was something special just because I was from Southern California. I knew I was different but never thought I was special. It was a wonderful break, because the entities that I was so familiar with in my house when I was younger seemed to be less common in the Midwestern town. They were still there, but not in the magnitude that they were in my house and family in California. It was one of the best summers of my life, since I spent most of my time fishing, but when the summer was over, I had to go back home.

The entities that I had known so well seemed to be waiting there to greet me. Most everything from my previous house hadn't made it to the apartment—I suppose because it was less room, and in truth, I still don't know where all those possessions of my childhood went. I had also been raising some pet lizards, and when I returned, they were dead on the patio, due to no food or water. My new stepmother would not allow them inside the house, so they were put on the patio to die. I assume everything else that was missing went in a dumpster.

Now began a new normal. I had a stepmom who had told me in so many words that I was not liked and was not welcome. She would use colorful metaphors with me, as was the custom in my house, but when my dad was there, she was nice. I didn't really understand why, but I guess she needed to put on a good face for my dad. My dad thought everything was wonderful and desperately wanted me to call my new stepmother Mom. My dad and I would get into many arguments over this. In private she would say things like "I'm not your mother, I don't want to be your mother, and even your own mother doesn't want to be your mother." This was in part a true statement, since at this time of my life I really didn't know where my mom was.

For some reason, when my dad was home, these entities were not as common. There were always one or two present in the room, but when he left on a job, the house seemed to be filled. Deception and hatred seemed to be most common, but still I had my verse: "The Lord is my shepherd, I shall not want, he leads me in paths of righteousness." And still there was this bubble around me. I felt safe and scared all at the same time when I was left with my stepmother. There was so much anger in her, so much bitterness and deceit. Up to this point in my life, I had known how to deal with people who were drunk or high, but I had never dealt with anybody who harbored so much anger and resentment. This was all new to me.

I think it was because I represented my mother, or maybe I just reminded her of a relationship that my dad had after leaving her the first time. Whatever the reason, it was obvious to me that the multiple entities following her about the house seemed to have a strong grasp on her. At times, I thought she knew they were there. She seemed to enjoy their presence, and there were times, especially when I would go to sleep, that I truly feared for my life. I just hoped that I would wake up in time. This went on for quite some time.

When I was between thirteen and fourteen years of age, I had an accident on the football field and needed medical care. My dad was out of town quite a lot, so I was left in the care of my stepmother. I had received a neck injury, and she would have to take me to see the doctor. In the beginning, she would take me, complaining all the way, with the entities following her in the car. It would feel so crowded in the car, as if there was not enough room for me. They were like luggage that she carried around with her all the time.

Later on, when she thought I was milking the situation, she would make me walk to the doctor's appointments, but I didn't mind; it was less crowded. I remember after the doctor's appointment, a nurse would see me walk to the parking lot but never go to a car. The next time I came in, they would inquire about it, but no one did anything other than ask.

Sometime that summer, my stepmonster, as she became known to me, said that her sons were going to come out and visit for the summer. Once again, my life was about to change, and now that I look back, I think it was to a degree planned. Not so much by my dad, but by my stepmother. My dad was on a job site, as always, leaving me in the care of my stepmonster. Her younger son and I got along well, while her older son didn't talk to me much. He had his eyes on my sisters. They were still hosting large parties with an assortment of drugs and alcohol. As strange as it was, I never took part in any of these things. Oh, I would go to the party, because I was considered, at fourteen years old, the "designated driver" before anybody coined that phrase. I was also introduced to my oldest brother, who turned out to be my half brother. He was my dad's son from his first marriage with my new stepmom. He and I would become friends. When I was kid, I always wanted a big brother, and he seemed to be nothing like his mom. He was like a lost friend that you found later on in life, and as the years went by, he and I became the best of friends.

My half brother was only able to stay in California for a short visit because he had brought his daughter with him. She was about four years old, sweet and wonderful to be around. My stepmother's younger son and middle son would stay with us for most of the summer. They seemed to fit in with my sisters very well, and all they wanted to do was party. I'm not sure if I went to all their parties, but there was a lot of partying going on. And the little entities that had been so prevalent throughout my life seemed to run rampant at these parties. As the night went on, they were getting drunker and drunker and higher and higher. My Psalm 23 verse still worked, even in these places. There was always a bubble around me, seemingly impenetrable to these entities, and in some ways, the people who were around me.

I remember people trying to hand me beers and marijuana cigarettes, and as strange as it may sound, whether it was one of my sisters, their friends, or a total stranger, somebody would always snap at the person trying to hand me the cigarettes or a bottle of beer. In my mind I was relieved, and I still wore my necklace that I had gotten when I was in kindergarten. At these parties I would watch these entities deceive people into doing things with other people as well as doing things to their own bodies that were destructive. I was still just a child put in some rough situations, but what these situations did for me was to make me more aware of the path I wanted to take. I would nearly vomit when I was around these types of parties. God had put his mark on me as a child. Even with these terrible entities surrounding me, I knew that my future would not be swayed by my current circumstances. This was all I knew: my seemingly endless journey through the valley of the shadow of death and that there was to be a light at the end of my tunnel—but not yet, not today.

Forced Independence

About this time, I started my working career, and in the early seventies, I began washing dishes at a well-known fast-food restaurant. My day would start early with either football or baseball practice. After practice, I would go to school, and when my school day was finished, I would go back to either football or baseball practice. Once that was done, I would ride my bicycle to the restaurant, where I was a p.m. prep and would prepare all the food for the following business day. I enjoyed what I did and took pride in my work. The demonic presence was still there, but as a general rule, they wouldn't bother me much. I think that when people are kept busy, these entities don't bother them nearly as much. It was mostly in people's idle time that they would stir and people allowed them to talk and would respond to what they whispered to them.

***

One of my short-term hobbies was BMX bikes. We had these large skate parks, and skateboarders as well as BMX bikers would do their best to hone their skills without breaking any bones. I was tall for my age but very skinny, and I had extremely good balance. The other kids I would see at the skate park were dealing with their own entities, but here fear wasn't one of them. It was most often a spirit of deception that would lead to marijuana or drug use. Because I was pretty good on my bike and they accepted me, I was able to talk to some of them about these entities, and in some cases, it seemed to help. I wouldn't tell them they were entities; I would just tell them that I felt like they were dealing with certain situations. They would respond with "Dude, does it show?" Or "Wow man, you must be reading my mind."

In most cases they wouldn't change anything in their lifestyle, but at least they were aware that it was noticeable to people around them, or at least to me. The guys who ran the skate park were cool and let me keep my BMX bike locked up with theirs in the building at the skate park; I would ride my beach cruiser to the park and then switch bikes. After I left the skate park, I would ride my bike home to meet the onslaught of demonic activity that had increased in my household.

Certain milestones in my life stand out more than others. Even though I have forgiven these things, I must remember my past because it is my testimony. A friend of mine says that the windshield on a car is large so that you can stay focused on where you're going, but the rearview mirror is small so that you can glance at it and have no doubt where you have come from.

Sometimes you get a chance to share your testimony with other people who are going through a similar circumstance. It can give them hope to remember that there is a valley of the shadow of death, but "Yea though I walk through the valley of the shadow of death, I will fear no evil: for thou art with me; thy rod and thy staff, they comfort me." (Psalm 23:4 KJV)

One day in the summertime, my stepmom's youngest son and middle son were with us at the apartment. My dad was on a construction job, so he was conveniently away from the apartment. One of my favorite things to do was cook French toast for breakfast. I would melt butter on the slices of toast and sprinkle powdered sugar on them instead of syrup. I made sure I made enough for my stepbrothers and my stepmother, but she would never eat my French toast. I was in the process of making my toast, so my stepbrothers were already eating.

The youngest son tended to eat with his mouth open, making a smacking noise. I never liked it, but for some reason, on that day, it made me slightly sick. I turned to see my stepmother sitting in our small living room and my stepbrother sitting at the table. I looked at the younger one and asked him to close his mouth when he ate. They both laughed, and then they both began to do it. My stepmother thought it was rather funny too, and I got mad and began to yell. The demonic entities in the house began to stir, flying around the room, and I knew that it probably had something to do with my anger and my stepfamily egging me on.

Within a few days of my French toast incident, my stepbrothers went back home to the Midwest. A few days after that, my stepmom told me, using many colorful metaphors, to pack up my stuff and get out of the house. I packed up what I could on my beach cruiser bicycle and left. I didn't have much, but I had a job, so I had money. I just needed a place to stay, but my mom's place was not an option. On the bright side, Southern California didn't get all that cold, and it was summertime.

I rode my bike to one of my friends' houses, on the same street we had just moved from. I sat on my bicycle in front of his house and really wasn't sure what to do. His dad scared me a little bit, and I wasn't sure I wanted to tell them what was going on. The high school I would be attending in the fall was just across the street. I was familiar with the school and knew that all I really needed was someplace to cover me from the sun in the daytime and from the occasional rain or wind. So I found a place at the high school where I felt I could hide, where no one would notice me. School was not in session, so I was able to go into places that would be hard to access during the school year. I was officially homeless, and I had only my belongings in the boxes that I had packed up before leaving the apartment for the last time.

I have had many silver linings throughout my life. They are not easily numbered. There are so many things to be thankful for, so many blessings bestowed upon me. I was about to receive a blessing from a very unexpected source. What I didn't realize was that there were janitors working on the school, painting, cleaning, repairing classrooms, and so on. I don't know if it was a janitor or my first encounter with an angel, but a man came up to me and asked me what I was doing. I had no idea in the world what to say, so I said nothing. He said, "Son, you can't stay here."

So I started packing up my stuff on the bicycle to figure out my next move.

He asked me, "Do you have any place to go?"

Again, I just looked at him and said nothing.

He helped me grab my boxes, and I pushed my bicycle. He said, "Come on" and led me to one of the janitor's rooms at the school. He said, "You can stay here for as long as you want, and I'll have a key made for you. There is a shower in the back for chemical emergencies. It only has cold water, but all you do is pull the chain if you need to use it. There are some army cots back here as well. I will have to show you how to put it together, because if anyone else comes in here and sees a cot set up, they may get suspicious. So you will have to put it away every morning." He asked me if I had a blanket and a pillow.

I said, "No, but I'll get one."

He gave me a key to his locker in the room and told me to stack my boxes in there. "And if anyone bothers you, tell them to come and talk to me."

I was so thankful. In the janitor's room, there were large washers and dryers for towels and sports uniforms. I would stand my bike up in the shower and pull the curtain closed in case somebody came in, so they wouldn't know anyone was there.

The checklist was being completed. I still had my job, I had money, I had clothes on my back, I had a mode of transportation, and now I had a place to park my bicycle, keep my boxes, and rest my head. I'm sure to most people this would seem pretty bad, but for the first time in my life, there were no entities around me; there was peace and light. There were no drugs, there was no alcohol, and there was no fear. I still didn't know God, but his presence, I believe, was always with me.

After the janitor left, I took my bicycle, rode to the nearest store, and bought a sleeping bag and a pillow. I also bought some dry food that I would keep in my box. When I came back from my shopping trip, my janitor friend was there, and he handed me a key that he had made. He said to me, "Use it whenever you want, for as long as you need."

I wanted to give him a hug but didn't know if that was the right thing to do. So I just shook his hand and said, "Thank you."

I found out later that my stepmother told my dad she had to kick me out of the house because she caught me having relations with another boy. Now, if you know my dad, he was an ex-navy man and a construction worker. If you wanted to push his buttons, you started talking about a boy having relations with another boy. I'm sure my stepmother knew this. She knew the right buttons to push, and my dad said something to the effect of "He's lucky I wasn't here. I would've killed them both."

It would be many years before I would see them again, and my dad and my stepmother moved back to the Midwest. I don't recall my dad saying anything to me, but eventually it was revealed that he was lied to about why I was kicked out of the house.

As for me, my life went on like normal—get up go to football/baseball practice, go to school, go back to football/baseball practice, go to work, return home to my janitor's room. I was very careful to make sure that nobody caught me coming in or out, but to be honest, if I was ever seen, nobody said anything to me. It became harder when school was getting ready to start. The teachers were coming to get their rooms ready, and I had to be very careful not be seen.

I had known kids who were in the foster care system, and that scared me because that wasn't where I wanted to end up. I liked where I was and would have been OK had it never changed. I would see my janitor friend from time to time, and we would just smile at each other. Sometimes he would ask me, when no one was around, if everything was going OK or if I needed anything. I would say, "No, I'm good. And by the way, thanks." He would just smile and go about his business.

I guess living out of the janitor's room for my four years of high school would have been a bit much to ask. I went to school and continued to get Cs, except for PE, where I always got As. I am not really sure how long I lived in the janitor's room at my high school, but it was close to a year. I guess at some point people started to get suspicious as to where I lived.

***

When my mother and father were married, we lived directly across the street from the high school I was attending, so when I would go to my friend's house, their parents would ask how my parents were doing, and of course, I would say, "They are doing fine." I never really mentioned they were divorced. In those days, you could keep things secret. In today's world, with social media, that would have been impossible.

I had a friend who worked at the same fast-food restaurant as I, and his family lived a short distance away from our high school. It was far enough away that his mom would have to give me a ride back to my house, or what she thought was my house. It was across the street from my janitor's room. I don't know how long she suspected I didn't live there, but one fateful day, she decided to watch me in the rearview mirror of her car. I would go to the door, as if to go in my old house, and wait there, waving goodbye as they went down the street and around the corner. It turned out she was a little smarter than I was, and as soon as she got out of sight, she turned around and came back. Obviously, I did not go into the house, and I was walking down the street.

She pulled up next to me and asked, "How come you didn't go in your house?"

I said, "Oh, I'm going to the school and ride around on my bike."

She said, "You don't live there anymore, do you?"

I had found out at a very early age that when I was confronted with questions, it was better to say nothing than to get myself in trouble, so I said nothing.

She asked, "Where are you living?"

I pointed at the school.

She asked if I had stuff there, and I said, "Yes."

She said, "Go get your stuff. You can stay with us."

Well, I wasn't going to argue, but I really liked staying in the janitor's closet. All I ever did there was sleep and shower. But now my secret was out, and for the time being, I would live at my friend's house, in an attic bedroom.

Chapter 3

My friend's house was so drastically different from where I had lived previously with my mom and dad and with my dad and stepmom. I think there were many times when I wished I could go back to the janitor's closet, but the proverbial cat was out of the bag, and my friend's mom was not going to have that. She was a bold person with a strong personality, but I never saw them do any drugs in the house and never sensed that that was taking place. They were more the type who would sip wine at dinner. I wasn't accustomed to that, because in the households that I had lived in, you would drink with a purpose, not to sip it with your dinner. They still used colorful metaphors here and there, and there was a strong sense of sexual tension in the house, but it was a change of scenery from the anger and fighting I was so used to.

I encountered something new and different at the hundred-year-old house where my friend's family lived. There had been terrible acts of violence performed both upstairs in the attic room, where I was staying, and in the basement, which connected to a type of catacomb that ran under the streets of the old California city. I was told that the tunnels met up with different missions and houses in the city.

I had never seen entities such as the ones I saw at this house, and because of the newness of them, they did frighten me a bit. But once I understood they were just like all the others, the shock wore off, and I became indifferent toward them.

When I was in my upstairs room by myself, these new entities would move slowly around the room to see if my eyes would follow them, and then they would look at one another as if to say, "He can see us." On one of the first nights I was there, I heard a thump in my room as I was sleeping. I was a light sleeper, and I woke up to see two entities that had somehow manifested themselves into larger forms about five feet tall. One of the entities was trying to say something to me, but once again, the only word I could make out was "seer." I had had some very short conversations with other entities previously, and it was as if they wanted me to do something.

The second entity, the one that was not trying to talk to me, walked over to the stairs, so I followed him. They motioned as if they wanted to walk down the stairs, so as I walked down the stairs, they followed me. This was a little strange, even for me; entities had followed me in the past, but these two seemed to want to follow me for a whole different reason. I kept sensing that they had never been out of the attic room, or at least not by way of the stairs that led to the main house. I didn't know how to play this, because I was pretty sure I would have no control over them once I opened the door to the second floor.

They had manifested themselves into what looked like deformed, hunchbacked persons, and this manifestation was new to me. When I opened the door and walked onto the second-floor landing, they stayed at the door to the attic and peeked around the corners, as if fearful of what they were seeing. One of them stepped out onto the landing, almost to where I was standing. The other one never left the doorway. And then, without any notice, they both went back upstairs. I followed them, and when I got back into the room, they were nowhere to be found.

The room that I stayed in was very strange, because the walls only went up about four or five feet, and then the ceiling peaked in the middle, so as to follow the roof line. The floor was covered with padded carpet, as well as some of the walls and part of the ceiling. There were parts of the wall that had wood planks.

***

After my third or fourth week of living at the house, one of the two entities I had seen earlier got my attention, walked over to a part of the wall that had the wood planks, and moved through the wall. I was a curious kid, so I went to the wall where the entity had moved through it. Another entity came up beside me and put his hand on the wall, as if to tell me to push. I pushed. Only about four planks moved, but they moved as one, so I pushed again, and still nothing. I then took my fingers and pulled the planks back toward me, and lo and behold, the wall had a door that opened to a very narrow staircase going down the side of the house between the inside wall and the exterior wall.

The steps were short and deep, but I was able to turn sideways and maneuver my way down with a flashlight, and it opened up in a part of the basement. I wasn't sure, but I didn't think you could access this room from the actual basement that the family used. There was a hinged door in the floor. When I opened it and shone my flashlight down, I saw a ladder. When I looked down into the passage, there were other entities looking up at me. I know it sounds weird, but I had gotten used to seeing these critters all the time, and they had never harmed me, so I was just curious.

I climbed down the ladder and into what I would later know as a type of catacomb. I thought this was crazy. I just stood there by the ladder, thinking if I were to follow these entities around these tunnels, the stupid little things would get me lost, and I might not be able to find my way back. I climbed back up the ladder, all the way up the stairs, back to my room, and closed the door in the wall.

On that following weekend, I asked my friend, "Do you know anything about tunnels under the house?"

He said that there were some newspaper clippings that talked about these catacombs. His family had seen them at the library in some of the archives. The articles spoke of their particular house and things that had happened here. He said that he knew of the articles but had never read them because things like that would freak him out. So his sister and stepbrother never brought it up. That would explain that spirit of fear that I had seen so many times in the house, a type of spirit of deception.

Later, to have a few hours by myself, I would tell the family that I was going for a jog or walk around the neighborhood. It was a big neighborhood and very old. The back fence where I stayed shared a wall with the old cemetery. I do not believe there were many people from the current century buried there, because it was full. Sometimes I would walk through the cemetery and see entities here and there, usually trying to provoke fear in me. Realizing I could see them and that they weren't affecting me, they would move along. I was just interested in reading the headstones. They were fascinating.

But sometimes, when I would tell my friend's family that I was going on these little journeys, in fact, I was going down the wall and into the catacombs. I seemed to get braver and braver, and the entities would try to coax me to go farther than I wanted. I would leave myself marks on the walls and carry extra batteries, just in case. I wasn't the first person to be down in these catacombs, and I was terrified that I would find somebody else down there with me. I really wasn't sure what went on down there, but on the occasion that I did see people, I would turn off my flashlight and just watch. Usually, it was kids drinking or doing drugs, but sometimes there were small groups of people down there doing things with strange chants. I didn't understand, but the entities that I had become so familiar with seemed to be gathered around these people, moving about the group as they chanted. The entities seemed to belong there with these people, and I always kept my distance.

I would also see graffiti that I didn't understand written or drawn on the walls. Some of the graffiti would have entities gathered around it, as if it was a focal point for them. Under my breath, just to be safe, I would utter my words from Psalm 23: "The Lord is my shepherd, I shall not want, he leads me in paths of righteousness." I didn't know why at the time, but saying these words always got their attention. I would say to myself, "You know they don't like it when you say that." But still, to this point, I had never looked into why they reacted to these words. I just knew the words worked, and they carried some type of power that I needed to calm myself.

One Friday night my friend and I decided to go on a double date, and I was very inexperienced at this. In fact, it may have been my first date. My friend's mom and dad both drove cars to the drive-in theater. Once we were parked side by side, my friend's mom got into the car with my friend's dad, and we got into the car with our dates. I didn't even know what movie we were going to see. I didn't go to movies much because it meant I would have to spend money that I didn't need to spend. But my friend's parents paid for the movie, so I thought, why not?

The movie turned out to be *Texas Chainsaw Massacre*. What a great first-date movie. Funny thing is, I couldn't really tell you much about the movie, because I didn't look at the screen. Oh, I know what you're thinking: that I was busy with the girl. Maybe that was the case in the backseat with my friend and his girlfriend, but in the front seat, there wasn't much going on. She watched the movie. I looked at everything going on in the drive-in other than what was on the screen. These little demonic entities were all over the drive-in, at least in the parts that I could see. They were on the cars, on the playground, under the big screen, next to us, behind us. It looked like an invasion. I thought, "You people are horrified at what you are seeing on the screen, but you have no idea what's going on all around you." For me, it was a milestone event that I didn't want to repeat ever again, and from that point on, I didn't like horror movies.

When we got home, my friend's parents asked me how I liked the movie and what I thought of this part or that part. I did what I always did best, which was to stay quiet, say nothing, and act as if I knew what they were talking about when, in fact, I knew absolutely nothing.

I found it fascinating that no one in the house other than my friend's parents would come up to my room. My best friend's sister and brother would not venture up the stairs to my room. I didn't really understand why they said it was too scary up there; I thought, "Oh, you mean the demonic entities that I share the room with? They're not so scary."

One day my friend and I both had a paper due, so we decided to go to the old library near his house. My papers usually weren't that good, so they didn't take very long. He was a much better student than I, and he would help me as much as he could. On this particular day, I finished early and asked him about the newspaper clippings that his mom and dad had spoken about concerning the house. Now, back in the old days, they had something called microfiche, which they would put all the old newspaper clippings on. The librarian helped me to find what I was looking for. The article said there had been twin boys living in the attic room that I was currently living in. The boys were considerably deformed, and at this time in history, they would hide or kill the deformed children. This family chose to hide them in the attic room.

This explained a lot to me, because the manifestations that I would see were all deformed. I also understood now why they were up there.

These entities seemed to like the darkness. Most of the time when I saw them, they were in the corners of the rooms or in shadowy places. They didn't seem to like the light very much. I saw them most often at night, and it seemed that in the catacombs, they felt safe. So it became clear to me why the room I lived in was set up the way it was and why these entities seemed to be so prevalent up there. I also understood why the three kids of the house didn't want to go up there.

My friend said, "You still want to sleep up there after reading the articles?"

I said, "Well, at least now I understand why you guys don't want to go up there."

I'm sure the kids couldn't understand why I could sleep up there, but I had been around these entities for most of my life, and they didn't seem to pose an actual threat to me physically, or at least not that I could tell. I slept just fine.

Back Home with Mom

I don't know how long I lived at my friend's house, but I know I spent one Christmas there. The reason I remember is because the Christmas tree was so big. The house had such high ceilings they needed ladders to decorate the tree, and even now, that memory has stuck in my mind. My friend's parents bought me gifts as if I were one of their own kids. I don't remember my father or mother buying me a gift that year.

In the spring of that year, I received word that my mother had gotten remarried. I hadn't seen her much since the divorce except that from time to time we would have lunch. It was always a little awkward because I didn't feel I knew her that well. The man she married was in the United States Air Force and was stationed at a base in the same city where I had been born.

He and my mom hadn't been married long, but he knew that his new wife had three daughters who were older and a son whom he assumed was older as well. I was told that he was very upset when he found out that I had been living with my friend's family.

So my mom scheduled a meeting for me to meet him. He was very nice to me, and while we were together, he asked if I would come live with him and my mom. I knew it must've been his idea, because I doubted it was my mom's. I went back to my friend's house and talked to his mom and dad, and they said they thought it would be a good thing if I went to live with my mother. I wasn't so sure. But I did know that sometimes it was awkward having me in their home, so I packed up what things I had and moved to my new stepdad's house with my mom.

It was a nice house, nicer than any house I'd ever been in. It had a hot tub and a barbecue grill in the backyard, with a pond and goldfish. I felt a little like the Beverly Hillbillies, going from living in the janitor's closet to a place like this, with my very own bedroom. My stepfather was nice—not very personable, but nice. He had a daughter who lived at the house who was one year older than I and a son who was in college. His daughter and I got along great, and his son as well. I truly think I felt closer to them than I did my own family, which didn't make sense. But for me it was the truth.

The demonic entities that I had dealt with for my entire life were less evident in this house. To my knowledge, my stepfather's daughter and son didn't have any entities following them around. I hadn't seen that very often. My stepfather did have an entity that stayed with him most of the time, because one of the biggest things that he and my mother had in common was their desire to drink alcohol and smoke cigarettes. I would consider both of them functioning alcoholics. My stepfather didn't ask me to call him Dad. He said that his first name would be fine.

***

I went to military functions at the air force base, and it was the first time I'd ever been around a military person or a military installation. This was new to me, and they all seemed to act like him. They would play softball, drink alcohol, and smoke cigarettes, but they seemed to have a wonderful time and liked being around one another a lot. When my mom got a little too much to drink, she would act silly and kind of flirtatious; my stepdad, on the other hand, was funny. He would be what you call a lovable, happy drunk. It was the only time he would hug me or tell me that he loved me, and I always knew when they were going to start drinking because the demonic entities would show up, and start moving about. Usually my stepsister would leave to go out with her friends. I would do the same, but I usually had practice, work, or homework.

I think my stepsister liked having me around. It was hard to tell, because she was a bit of a tomboy as well as a very good soccer player in high school. But she was also like her dad and didn't show her emotions a lot.

Her friends would come around, and even though I was very shy and never went out of my way to chase her friends, they seemed to like me. When I wasn't in school, at baseball or football practice, or working at the restaurant, I had a mild addiction to working out with weights. My stepsister's friends were fascinated by this and would come over often to watch me. I thought lifting weights was great; it was usually something I did all by myself, but having people watch me made me push a little harder.

***

Living with my stepdad and mom was probably the best time of my life to this point. I never felt fearful, and for the first time in my life, I had a relationship with my mom. When I was a kid playing sports, my dad always seemed to be there, whether he was my coach or just a helper. He enjoyed being around the sports environment. I think he knew that academically speaking, I was never going to be an Einstein, but in sports, it was a level playing field for me, one that I excelled in. Maybe I had a little bit of an advantage, but as far as everyone else knew, it was a level playing field. One time a teacher told me, "It's a good thing you're good at sports, because you're not very good at much else."

***

My stepdad and my mom attended many social events, so many that I couldn't count them. They would start off with these entities seeming to egg them on to drink more and more. Then the entities would show up in greater numbers, and I knew that things would start to escalate. I would generally leave the house and walk around the neighborhood. It was so peaceful, with the smell of orange blossoms, palm trees swaying, and yes, sometimes the smell of smog, if the wind was blowing just right.

At one such gathering that my stepdad and mom hosted at our house, I went out to the garage with my cement weights, turned the radio on, and worked out, just for something to keep my mind occupied. At some point, I went back into the house with all the intoxicated people, and if I had been smart, I would have put something over my nose and mouth, because the smoke was so thick. Even with all the smoke, I could still smell something different. You're probably thinking it was drugs, but it wasn't; it just smelled funny. I followed the smell to the laundry room. My mom, who was very much intoxicated, had been doing laundry. When I opened the door, the odor was very strong. The cat had unfortunately jumped into the dryer with the warm clothes and had been asleep when my mom went in to fluff the clothes. I opened the door to the dryer, and out came all this fur. No, the cat did not survive. I took our cat out of the dryer, wrapped him in a sheet, and took him out to the garage. The next day we were all sad and had to clean the dryer. I guess it's the price you pay when you drink to the point of not knowing what you're doing.

***

By this time, when I walked past the janitor's closet, I would feel the key in my pocket, look in, and think about living there; it wasn't so bad. I would look for the janitor who had given me the key and allowed me to stay there, but after that summer, I never saw him again. I wish I had known his name. I'm sure there was a name tag on his coveralls, but either he was an angel manifested to protect me or just an incredible person whom God had put in my path to be a blessing. It's not as if I would walk past the room and tell my friends, "Hey I used to live there." It would be my secret, shared only with my friend and his mom.

In high school, unlike elementary school, there were sometimes more of these entities present than there were people in the school. I guess in elementary school, kids are more innocent and have less going on, and I'm sure they have far fewer worries about the events of the day. In elementary school, we didn't really think much about being shot or stabbed, or what party we would be going to that night, and I really wish that girl liked me, or the fact that I need to keep my grades up so I can get into a good college. Yes, in elementary school, there was a lot less peer pressure.

In junior high school, it was a little more intense, and the entities started showing up more often. They appeared through the power of suggestion and had the ability to start fights and depress people; it all started to be a real thing. Peer groups were formed at this time. You were either one of the smart people, a jock, a druggie, or, in some situations, a gang member. I suppose everyone else was just trying to figure out where they fit in. These entities that I had become so used to were never far away.

For whatever reason, I fit into a few of the social categories quite seamlessly. I knew most of the druggies by way of association, and they all knew my sisters because of their older siblings. The smart people knew me because in athletics, they are the people cheering you on at the games and wishing they had the athletic ability the jocks possessed. Even the gang members came to football games and would, in their own way, cheer for their high school team, although they had already dropped out or graduated.

It was here in high school that I began to recognize the entities that I had seen with people and the negative effects that they would have on them.

***

For me, just over my own shoulder, I had no doubt that entity of fear was breathing down my neck as well—fear that I would be made fun of for my schoolwork, fear that even though all my friends would be going to college, it might not be in the cards for me. I had a very real fear of parties and all the activities that went along with them. I wanted to fit in, but something in my spirit said, "Not at all costs." The entity of fear that followed me around would tell me that I would never measure up, never be like one of the cool kids. I was able to see these entities with other people, but until high school, I was blind to my own fears. I remember the pressure that I would feel in classrooms when the teacher called on me. The kids who had been in school with me for years knew that I was not the sharpest tool in the shed.

But this was high school, and not everybody had been in school with me for years. When I was a freshman, there were three junior high schools that came together into one high school, so people who knew me as an athlete did not know me as a student.

Sometimes the pressure was so great that I could almost feel the entity breathing down my neck. The entity of fear would grip me, and I would freeze as the teacher said my name and then waited for me to answer a question or read out of a book. I would resort back to my earlier theory, which was, if you don't know the answer or can't perform the task, say nothing! Sometimes the teachers were persistent and would ask me again and again. I felt as if my head was going to explode, as this entity would speak into my ear.

I would try to quiet the entity by doing the only thing I knew to do: Psalm 23. "The Lord is my shepherd, I shall not want, he leads me in paths of righteousness." Again and again I would say this to myself.

The teacher would say, "We can't hear you; can you please speak a little louder?"

I would say to myself, "You wouldn't understand."

It got to a point where I was more conscious of the entities around me than I was of the entities around other people. I was used to being entertained by things going on around me, but now, it was I who was the entertainment.

***

I had never been taught to pray at that point in my life, but if I had known how, my most frequent prayer would have been "Please don't call on me in class. Amen." I would watch the entities move about the room when the teacher called on other people, but unlike before, my heart would go out to them.

I look back and wish I had known the power of prayer, but at this time in my life, that was a complete mystery to me. Most of the time, it would feel as if I were holding my breath while I was in class, and the second I walked out that classroom door, I could breathe again. We had an open campus, and each building had four classrooms and sidewalks connecting them. Most had little awnings over the sidewalks so that we wouldn't get wet when it rained. I would walk to my next class and notice my classmates at their lockers, walking to their next class, and standing and talking to their friends, and the entities would sometimes make eye contact with me, as if to say, "I know you can see me, but what good does that do? They won't believe you anyway." And they would go back to what they were doing. I guess I didn't care enough to say anything at this point in my life. I was dealing with my own entities, my own shortcomings, my own fears.

Using Fear as My Ally

In baseball my ninth-grade year, many of the people I had played Little League and Senior League with were there, and on the baseball diamond, fear was still my ally. I could still use fear in the same way I used a curveball or a changeup. I had no fastballs, but as long as their fear was my friend, I could still perform at a high level, to the joy of my coaches. I had also found out that when I came to the plate to bat, I could envision myself hitting the ball. I never allowed myself to see anything else. I never allowed that entity of fear to come anywhere close to me, and if I felt it at all, I would back out of the batter's box, kick some dirt, take a couple of swings, get my head back on straight, and go back to the plate. I had no question in my mind that I could not be struck out. I knew what I had seen for years, with all the batters who faced me, and I knew why they were unable to hit my pitches. I knew I could control it, but I did not come to this revelation until my freshman year. From that point on, I could hit with the best of them and became a sought-after player.

In football, the ability to see these entities didn't have the advantages that it had in baseball. In baseball, you are standing at the plate by yourself, or you are in a field position by yourself, and the team, as a whole, can't help you. But football is more of a team sport. You have to depend on other people to do their jobs in order to be successful. You could have one great player on a bad team, and you are still going to lose.

I would see the entities on the field with certain players, but I was a wide receiver, and fear was not really a part of my game. In fact, fear was a motivator in the position I played because I did not like being hit. To counter that, I would run fast. I wasn't sure how the ability to see these entities would play a role in football, but sometimes I would feel the presence of an entity with the kid who was supposed to be guarding me, and since I was a quiet kid, I didn't talk much trash. I found out that most of the kids who did talk trash were afraid, and that was a huge advantage for me.

Occasionally, after a game, I was asked to go to parties, usually with other baseball or football players. I would weasel my way out of going. My schedule was still as tight as before: school, practice, work, and then home. In the case that a cute girl would invite me, I would sometimes go, but it wouldn't take long before they realized I wasn't the partying type. People knew who I was because I was good in sports. Most guys who were athletes also knew how to party. This was the reason athletes and potheads knew each other. The funny thing was, when I would get to the parties, the potheads already knew I wouldn't partake, and the unseen entities knew as well and would leave me alone. Most of the girls were turned off by my lack of desire to get drunk or high. This would follow me throughout my high school career, as I didn't date much. Most of the people I went to school with didn't know me very well, but I had good friends whom I worked with. None of my coworkers went to my school, so they only knew me as a coworker or an athlete.

***

I was a very hard worker, and most of the time when we were working, the entities didn't show up. There was the occasional person who was angry with someone else, and I could see the entities between them, but most of the time, we were all like family. Not a family that yelled at one another, but a family that liked being around one another. Sometimes, in our off-hours, we would hang out with one another outside the store in the parking lot, or, on occasion, go someplace else. This was when the entities would show up. Sometimes, my coworkers would smoke pot, and usually there was alcohol, so I would carry around my familiar little red cup to fit in. I felt as if I had danced this dance so many times in my life, and it had become so familiar to me. By this point in my life, I had connected these entities with partying, anger, depression, and fear. I'm sure the list could go on, but it seemed to be always the same thing, and still I didn't understand it.

I look back and think about all the pressures a kid has going on in the first year of high school. I was no different; I really wanted to tell people what I was seeing with them, these entities that would show up at strategic times. I really wanted to say something, to see if I could possibly change the outcome or maybe defuse a situation, but sadly, I stayed quiet and said nothing. I would just watch things unfold. I never wanted to see anybody get hurt, and sometimes I would feel bad and think, "I should've said something." These were often my friends, my family, my classmates, or my coworkers. These thoughts would weigh heavy on my heart and mind for many years to come, but obviously not heavy enough. I had dealt with enough humiliation in classrooms, and when I was a child, my family thought I had mental issues and gave me medication. I could not risk being taken out of sports or losing my friends and job. I saw no upside to telling them what I could see around them.

I didn't feel I could make a difference by bringing it up, because no one would believe me anyway.

So here I was, in high school, and still had "imaginary" friends. I felt that giving out this information would be disastrous for my social situation, so why risk it? As always, I just stayed quiet.

***

One night after work at the fast-food restaurant, my friends wanted to go to a late movie. It was a Saturday night, so there was no football the next day, no practice, and no school. I thought, sure, why not? A small group of us all jumped into one car. I think there were five or six of us. We would usually go to a drive-in, but the cinema was where we ended up. Walking up to the doors, I still didn't know what show we were going to see, but I was with my friends, so I was going to go along with it anyway. I remember this event well because at that time, I had told myself I would never go to another scary movie. But here I was, with my friends, and peer pressure does intimidate you to do things you really don't want to do.

The movie was *The Exorcist*, and I thought, "No big deal. I'll just stare under the screen like I have done in the past." The thought of this made me want to throw up, and the reason this movie would stay etched in my mind was because I didn't go to the cinema very often. I was frugal with my money. We could pile more people into a car and go to the drive-in much cheaper.

We bought our tickets, walked in, and chose seats in the back of the theater, because one of the guys thought he was going to be making out with the girls who were with us. I was sure this would turn out to be a mistake for us all and me especially.

Before the movie even started, I could see entities of fear all over the room. Some were even hanging from the sides of the walls. I couldn't tell where they were coming from, but they seemed to be anticipating this particular movie. The lights dimmed, and the projector started. The only entities I could see were the ones closest to me, and as my eyes adjusted, I could see them everywhere. Some of these chimpanzee-sized entities, horribly disfigured, were hanging off the backs of people's chairs, while others were almost sitting in their laps. My plan to stare underneath the screen was not going to work this time. I wasn't sure why I was scared. After all, it was just a movie, and they were just actors, I told myself. I turned to the only thing I knew: my magic bullet that seemed to never fail me. I turned to Psalm 23 and spoke the verse under my breath, so not to be heard by my friends sitting beside me.

It was like nothing I had ever seen before, and I had seen a lot of things. If I had known what I know now, I would've thought that I was in some compartment of hell. But no, I was just in a movie theater. About halfway through the movie, most everyone was experiencing some type of fear. These entities had wreaked havoc on people's thoughts during this movie. The only redeeming factor was that a fairly cute girl had decided to bury her face in my shoulder and would ask me after a few minutes if it was OK for her to look again. Little did she know, I still had not looked at the screen, so I had no idea what to tell her. I glanced up for a split second, looked back down toward my feet, and said to her, "Nope, don't look yet." I really didn't know what was going on in the movie, but I did know I liked her leaning into my arm like that, and she smelled better than the guy on my other side, who had been cooking burgers the entire night and smelled like fast food.

Did I mention this was about a two-hour movie? Unfortunately for me, the girl's courage came back to her, and she went back to watching the movie. The guy on the other side, at one point, asked me if I was OK. I thought, "I must be saying my verse a little too loud."

The one thing I would take from this event was that as I said my verse under my breath, even though fear was all around me and even upon me at times, I could regain my courage. As I started reciting my verse again, the bubble of protection would form around me. You would think that by now I would've researched this verse and actually picked up a Bible and looked up Psalm 23, but except for an occasional Sunday-school class, where I was sometimes made fun of for my lack of reading skills, I had never even picked up a Bible. I had no idea where you would even get one.

At last, this marathon of fear was over, and as most people do, my friends walked out of the theater talking about the movie. I did what I had always done when I had no idea what the answers to the test were. I just stayed quiet until I had enough information, by way of listening to them, that I could formulate my own answers and not look stupid, pretending I had watched the whole movie.

It was quite some time before I would ever go back into a movie theater again. Just the thought of all those entities climbing on the walls and seemingly coming out of the floors made me not want to go back anytime soon.

When I returned home, my stepsister asked, "What movie did you see?"

I said, "*The Exorcist*" and "if you are smart, you will never go see it."

She just laughed.

***

By this time in my life, I was seeing the entities daily. It was during group activities that I would see them on a larger scale. Because it made me uncomfortable, I would walk away from whatever it was they were doing. My middle sister still lived nearby, and sometimes I would go over to visit her. The apartment complex she lived in had a pool. They would throw parties, starting off just drinking beer, but before long, they would break out the pot, and then it was just a show for me.

I knew that the entities would soon show up, and as always, they didn't disappoint. The parties would get crazier and crazier. Fortunately for me, they would usually smoke pot in the backyard. In the midseventies, I don't think anyone thought much about secondhand smoke inhalation. By the end of the night, the party would have moved to the common area of the apartment complex and the pool. Bathing suits were optional, but when it's your sister skinny dipping, it isn't exciting; it's just weird. My older sister also lived in the area. I guess she took on a big-sister approach, and she didn't like her friends or boyfriend or husband, whichever the case was, to smoke pot or do drugs around me; just cigarettes and beer.

As I said before, my sisters were protective of me, even when I was a teenager, but my oldest sister was the most protective. It was as if she could see things in me that I didn't see in myself. Somehow, I think she knew that I would break out of the world I had grown accustomed to and held me to a different standard than my other two sisters or even my parents. She knew I was going to turn out different from the rest of my family.

Chapter 4

As I came into my sophomore year of high school, baseball started again. The entity of fear that I had used to get an edge on batters seemed to be diminishing. It wasn't that my ability to see them went away, but the batters had become increasingly less fearful of what I was able to do as a pitcher. I noticed that pitchers with a great fastball seemed to enhance the entities of fear, but all I had was a curveball. There were still the occasional batters I could intimidate with a great breaking ball, but most had seen it enough that their coaches made sure they were ready for it. I had played catcher and shortstop before, but I was known as a pitcher. I had never played these other positions at the high school level. I decided to concentrate more on my batting and become a better catcher. As a catcher, I could still utilize my abilities to sense or see fear in a batter. I had pitched enough to know what would work and what wouldn't work on a specific batter. I was still cheating, but from a different viewpoint on the field, and in my own mind, I patted myself on the back for finding out a whole new way to use this gift.

School was still school. I could go on and on about fear gripping me in the classroom, but in that aspect, some things had never changed.

In my secondary sport, football, I would learn a new way to play the game. One day in football practice, our JV team was practicing kickoffs and returns, and they decided to put me on the kickoff team. The kicker put the ball in the air, and I ran down the field. I'm sure on paper this doesn't sound all that impressive, but when I tackled the kid who caught the ball, the coaches were impressed. They yelled at the kickoff return team for failing to stop me and allowing the kickoff return guy to be hit like a tidal wave. They shouted, "Line it up again. Let's do it over."

I thought, "This is kind of fun." For once in my life in the game of football, I didn't really have to worry about somebody tackling me. As receiver, I would catch the ball, and fear was the great motivator to run fast. This was different; instead of being the one who was running in fear, I realized that creating the fear, as I had done in baseball for so many years, played right into my hand.

So once again the kicker put the ball in the air, and once again I was able to make the play on the young man receiving the ball. The next thing I knew, our starting kickoff return team was running laps while the coaches called me over to talk. From that point on, I was no longer going to be a wide receiver. I was going to do something a lot more fun, using my specific gift of identifying entities of fear to my advantage. That season I would start on the kickoff team. I had never played much defense, but from here on out, I was destined to play defensive end.

At that point in time, I don't remember seeing the entity of fear in the beginning of the game. I wasn't all that big, and as much as I lifted weights, I wasn't all that strong; but speed and quick reflexes were attributes that I did possess, and I would use them often at my new position. When we were being issued our equipment, I would make sure to get the biggest pair of shoulder pads I could find, anything that would make me look bigger.

During this year, I went from being known for my baseball skills to being noticed on the football field. Always before, having the ability to use somebody else's fear in football had never really worked for me, but now at this new position, I felt like a kid with a new toy. I truly believe that we all have God-given gifts. I think we have the ability to choose whether to use those gifts to honor God, honor the world, or, which is usually the case, honor ourselves. I believe most people bury their God-given gifts, and they go on with their lives, and the world never even knows they possess a gift. I also believe that we come to a crossroads in our lives, a path that is before us, and we are faced with the choice to follow the light of God or to follow the world into darkness. God gave us free will. I had not yet come to my crossroads, and I was still trying to figure out my path in this world, but soon I would be faced with a decision that would put me on a collision course with my Lord and Savior.

***

As you can tell, I didn't really have any close friends. I had many friends and really no enemies. I was the type of guy who got along with most everyone; being quiet and shy made me agreeable to pretty much everyone. I believe in high school I had only one actual girlfriend. She didn't go to my school, and I met her through a friend I worked with. God had given me the ability to just listen, so I had many friends who were girls, and because I had this ability to just listen, they enjoyed using me to vent their problems. All kinds of problems— problems with their friends, problems with their boyfriends, problems with their parents. Yes, God had given me this incredible gift, and at times it really didn't feel like a gift: to just listen. I would hear things like "I wish my boyfriend would just listen like you." The voice in my mind would say, "I really wish you would stop talking because you're making me late for class." Sometimes I just wanted to run away, but I just sat there listening.

My stepdad and mom thought I was juggling all these girlfriends at the same time, but nope, not the case. My stepsister thought it was hilarious and would say things like "Have you ever thought about asking any of these girls out?" I would think, "I think about a lot of things; I just don't say anything."

Luckily for me, my actual girlfriend went to a different high school, so when these girls would call me and talk to me, it didn't bother her at all, since there was no social media. "Glory to God in the highest."

***

My girlfriend and I had a pretty safe relationship; the one thing that stands out to me most was her house. She lived in a trailer house in a very upscale trailer park. When we think of a trailer park, the word *upscale* doesn't really fit, but this place was incredible. It had beautiful tennis courts and swimming pools, and it was nicely landscaped and well kept—not your everyday trailer park. My girlfriend's mother was divorced; it always scared me a little bit when we went to her house because I could see this entity following my girlfriend's mom around the house. I wasn't afraid of her mom because she was mean or hateful. On the contrary, she thought I was the most wonderful guy in the world. But I wasn't sure that her intentions toward me were purely innocent, so I would spend as little time as possible at her house, especially when her mom was home.

I never saw any entities with my girlfriend. She was an incredible person and, at that time in my life, a great friend. For all the activities I had going on in my life, I felt as if I were secluded on an island. At no time in high school did I ever mention or give any indication about what was once called my imaginary friends. It was as if the entities wanted me to feel they were the only ones that knew I could see into this other dimension. I would question myself and wonder if there was something really wrong with me. No one else could see these entities. Did they really exist? Should I reach out and ask for help or just continue on my path of silence? I would hold fast to the words I had repeated again and again for so long: "The Lord is my shepherd, I shall not want; he leads me in the paths of righteousness." In my mind this verse was the only thing that had brought me comfort and safety when I needed it, and it had created a bubble that would somehow encapsulate me. I still did not understand the words, but I knew the effect they had was real, and I could trust in them.

***

As I started my junior year in high school, the entity of fear that I knew was close beside me became much more real. I had no idea in the world what I wanted to do with my future. All I knew at that time was I did not want to go into the military like my stepfather. I don't know if it was because of how the military was perceived in the sixties and seventies, but in my mind, that was not a path I wanted to take.

In my baseball career that year, I started the transition from pitcher to catcher, and my ability to see into the spirit realm was still beneficial, so much so that I was noticed by a minor-league scout for both my pitching and catching, not to mention my hitting abilities. I believe most people thought I would go on to play baseball, whether in the minor leagues or beyond. I hoped that as well, because for me college was a scary option, and working in fast food for the rest of my life didn't seem like the answer. All my hopes and dreams were on baseball.

At home, life went on as usual. We ate well because my stepdad enjoyed grilling steaks, and I enjoyed eating them. There was always plenty of beer, vodka, and cigarettes, but I was never tempted to experiment with any of them. I guess I had already witnessed where those roads led, and I had no desire to travel down that path. I kept lifting weights, but I could not afford those fancy new protein powders, so my stepdad would buy cases of eggs at the commissary (military grocery store). After lifting weights each day, I would eat one dozen raw eggs and chase them with a glass of orange juice. I enjoyed working out, and it took my mind away from everything else. It was one of the few times in my day when I felt absolute peace.

***

After a varsity football game my junior year, when I had scored two touchdowns, my teammates insisted I go out to party. To make sure I went, two of my friends followed me to my house so I could drop off my car, and they were to escort me personally to the party. Now, when I went to parties at my sister's house, there was an understanding with all their friends that they were not to put any pressure on me to partake in any of the partying festivities, if you know what I mean. But this was not one of my sister's parties, and there was no understanding with my friends that I would not be partaking with them. I'm sure my imagination ran wild, but I knew that there was going to be quite a bit of drinking and smoking and then whatever would take place after that.

***

Something inside me told me that I needed to get out of this situation. As I dropped off my car, I told my two friends that I had to go to the house for a second. They said, "Make it fast." So I went to the door and faked a conversation with my stepdad at the front door. In this fake conversation, he insisted that I get into the house now. I think back on this, and I have to laugh; luckily my friends bought the story hook, line, and sinker. I know it was a flat-out lie and my friends just wanted me to enjoy myself and show me some appreciation, but the fact was, my stepdad and mom were not even home. They were at a party themselves.

As I walked into the house, my stepsister asked me whom I had been talking to. I told her "Nobody" and laughed under my breath, with a sigh of relief.

The next day, one of my friends who was with me that night said that they were afraid that my stepdad was going to come out and talk to them. They knew he was a military man and were afraid of him. I'm not sure why, because he wasn't a mean person, but maybe they didn't know that.

Demonic Manifestation

At this point in my life, my routine was consistent. In the summer I would work as many hours as I could and try to save the money. Toward the end of summer, varsity football two-a-days would start, then school, and sometime after Christmas break, baseball would begin. My senior year would produce an outcome that would make me change how I looked at my future. I don't know if it was the stress of pitching or the repetitive throws of playing catcher, but I injured my throwing arm. If million-to-one odds at making it in baseball wasn't enough now, I couldn't throw a baseball without being in a lot of pain. Whatever had happened, it wasn't healing very quickly, and soon the scouts or the minor-league baseball teams would pull back their offers.

The entities that had created so much fear for me in the classrooms were now telling me my future was looking very dim. All I had left was my fast-food career, where I had been promoted to assistant manager. By this time, I had been working there for four years, and I thought at least I had a job. My stepdad kept pushing me to check out the military, but I still didn't feel it was a viable option for me. The fear and desperation as to what I was going to do after high school would become a heavy burden for me to carry around. I felt the weight of it each and every day.

***

One evening while I was working at the restaurant, a friend told me there was a church in town that was putting on free Christian concerts. I thought, "Wow, that's great. Why are you telling me this?" He said that it was one of the really big churches in town, and there were a ton of girls there. In my mind, free was good, and being surrounded by a lot of teenage girls was even better. Being the good boyfriend, I asked my girlfriend if she wanted to come to the concert with me. She said it wasn't her sort of thing and to go ahead and go without her. I asked where this church was and when they were doing this. I didn't really know much about church, just that I hadn't really ever been to one, so he and I decided to go together.

When we arrived, he was right. There were a lot of people. I would guess somewhere near two thousand or three thousand people, and at least half were teenage girls. I was not really paying much attention to the music or what was being said. I just liked being around all those girls. Looking back, I was in the right place for the wrong reason, but I think the way God looked at it was that I was there, in church and for the first time enjoying it. I think that first night I was a bit overwhelmed, and I had no idea what to think or what was going to happen. Was it going to be church as I had always known? Was I going to have to read out loud? It was nothing like that. We were jumping around and dancing in the aisle. If there were any spiritual entities in the building, I wasn't aware of it. Of course, all I was used to seeing were these small entities that seemed to bring bad news to everyone they encountered.

***

The following week, my girlfriend and I decided to go for a drive in a famous part of the Hollywood Hills. I knew exactly where I wanted to go, because I had mapped out the area a few days earlier. As far as she was concerned, we were just going for a random drive to see some of the lights of the city from a great vantage point. I had found a place where they were starting to build some houses. The ground work was mostly finished, so it was very flat and easy to get into. They hadn't paved the road yet, so it was still marked out with flags, and there were some concrete gutters that had been put in place. It had been very dry, so when I drove out to where I wanted to park with my girlfriend, it was very easy to see my tracks.

    We pulled into a developing housing tract that had a great view of the city lights. To my right and left, all I could see was house pads being built, and behind me, on the other side of the street, more house pads. After I parked the car and turned off my lights, my girlfriend marveled at the view of the city and asked me how I knew about this spot. I was honest with her and told her that I had come out there earlier in the week and just stumbled upon it.

At that moment I wasn't thinking about seeing anything in the spirit. All I was thinking about was this great spot with a great view, and I had a very attractive girl sitting in the car next to me.

We started to kiss, and then I heard a banging noise on the top of my car, which stopped the kissing rather quickly. As I looked past my girlfriend's head, there appeared to be a man standing on the passenger side of my car; it was a full moon that night, so I could see pretty well. He had dark hair and a red shirt and white pants on. He yelled from the passenger side and told us to get out of the car.

I told him, "I'm not getting out of the car, but if we're not supposed to be here, we will go ahead and leave."

He banged on the top of my car again and then showed me some type of handgun that he was holding, and once again he said, "Get out of the car!"

My girlfriend was starting to cry and said to me, "I don't want to get out of the car. I think he's going to kill us!"

I looked back at the man standing at the passenger window with his face very near to the glass, and for a split second, I felt sure that this was no man, but somehow an entity that had manifested itself to look different. Up to this point in my life, I had never heard of anything like that, nor had I ever seen it happen. But in my mind, I felt sure that this was all some sort of illusion. So I yelled back to him and said, "We're not getting out of this car, so if you are going to shoot us, you will have to do it through the window." I also said, "I am going to start this car and put it in reverse, back out of this parking spot, and leave. There is really nothing I can do to stop you, but I can do my best to leave."

Again, he banged on the top of my car with the handle of his gun and once again said, "Get out of the car, now!"

With that, I started my engine, looked down at my gear shifter, and put the car in reverse. When I looked up, he was still standing there with the gun in his hand. I started backing up, and when I got to the street and put my car in drive, I looked up again, and he was still standing in the same spot, with the gun pointed at my car. Now, I had a pretty fast car, but I knew that if I put my foot into the gas, all I was going to do was spin my tires in the dirt, so I drove out slowly until I hit some asphalt, and then we were out of there.

Of course, my girlfriend said we would never do that again, and she was right. We never did. When we got to her house, she was still pretty shaken up. I walked around the car to the passenger side and put my arms around her to try to calm her down, and I noticed that there were a few chips in the paint on the top of the car, as well as one or two very small dents on the passenger side. This took place on a Friday night, so the next day I called her and said, "I want to go back out in the daylight to where we were last night and look around."

She said, "I think you're crazy, but I'll go with you."

So we went out to the same spot, and I was as careful as I could be to drive in the same tracks that I had made the night before. I stopped the car about ten feet from where I had parked the night before. Since it was so dry again, it was easy to see my tire tracks in the daylight. My girlfriend didn't want to get out of the car. She thought I was stupid for even going back, but I had a hunch of what I might see, and I had to find out.

When I got out of the car, I was careful to walk as softly as possible. When I came to the place where my car had stopped the last night, I looked on what would have been the passenger side of the car, and what I saw made very little sense. I could see footsteps where the man had been standing on the passenger side of my car, and his feet had been shuffling around, but there were no footprints walking in or out from the side of my car. Unless he came in on the top of my car, which would've been very hard to do without me knowing it, he had just manifested in that spot for some unknown reason. What he was going to do with us if we had gotten out of the car is still unknown.

***

I believe this was the first time in my life that an entity had manifested to me in a normal human form. Maybe it was because I had started going to church, and the deceiver wanted to change my path. I suppose I will never know, but I did know that my girlfriend never wanted to go for a drive with me to an unknown destination again. Not long after that, we started to go down different paths, and I didn't see her much anymore. Maybe it was our encounter in the Hollywood Hills, or the fact that I started going to church. She didn't really know what to think about that. We were still friends and would talk, but our dating relationship had come to an end.

Angelic Revelation

I kept going to the Christian music concerts at the church. Sometime after the third concert, my friends and I actually started paying attention to what they were saying. We became friends with some of the people we had seen there. At the end of each concert, they would have an altar call and would invite people to come up front and give their lives to the Lord. I had to talk to some of the people around me to understand what that meant. After they clarified this, I felt I needed more information before I went up front, but at that third concert, I felt a tug on my heart that I hadn't felt before.

The concerts were on Friday nights, and since it was no longer football season, I could generally go to them, and they always talked about church on Sunday morning. I didn't tell my friend, but I wanted to see what that was like. So that following Sunday, I decided I was going to go to the big church on the hill. They had three services every Sunday. I parked my car and was walking through the parking lot to the front doors. I was about a hundred feet from the church, and there were three or four sets of double doors with greeters who would shake your hand and say good morning as people were coming into the church.

I came to a stop at about fifty feet before the doors. I could see standing behind each set of greeters a very large person, ten to twelve feet tall, and as people walked through the doors on their right and on their left, they would reach out their hand and touch them on their head. Now, I had seen the little entities my entire life, but I had never seen anything like this.

People were just walking past me. I was like a small tree planted in an inconvenient spot, making people walk around me. I don't really know how long I stood there, but it was long enough to draw some attention. At that point, I started walking toward the door, but I was not making eye contact with the greeters at the doors. I was looking at this large fellow standing behind him and wondering what in the world this was.

Without me even looking at the greeter, he said, "Son, do you see something?"

I glanced at him and said, "Nope."

He said, "You do see something, don't you?"

All I could think about was my childhood and the fact that this could turn out badly; they probably had the medication right there in the building. I did not give him a reply. In my world, saying nothing was better than saying something that would make me look stupid.

He said, "Wait right here. I want you to tell somebody what it is you're seeing."

I wanted to ask if the person was a psychologist—I've already talked to one of those, and I won't take the pills. Just saying.

A minute or two later, a burly man showed up. His hair was somewhat long, like mine, but he was older and had a beard. He said, "So tell me what you saw."

I just looked at him as if to say, I have no idea what you're talking about.

He said, "How tall do you think he is? Ten or twelve feet?"

I looked at him in amazement, and I choked out the words "Can you see them? Can everyone see them?"

He said, "No, I have never seen them, but people have told me about them. Can you describe them to me?"

I said, "Only if you can tell me what they are."

He pulled me off to one side and said, "I'm thinking you have a gift, but you have no idea what it is."

All I wanted to know was who these guys were that stood ten to twelve feet tall.

At last he said, "Those are angels. Have you ever seen one before?"

I just looked at him and said, "No. I only know the little small chimpanzee-looking things."

He said, "So, how often do you see these demons?"

I thought, "So that's what they are." I said, "Demons. So, you're telling me those little entities are demons, and the tall ones are angels."

He smiled and said, "Son, you and I have a lot to talk about."

I said, "I really just wanted to come to church."

He said, "You go to church, and if you see anything, you tell one of the ushers to come tell me. I want to hear all about it."

I had a secret that I wasn't allowed to tell anyone, and for the first time in seventeen years, the first time in my life, someone wanted to hear about it. In that moment, my entire life changed. Someone wanted to hear about what I was seeing without thinking I was crazy or that I needed medication. Someone didn't think I was lying or just trying to get attention in this area of my life that I had kept secret for so long. Someone was telling me that what I was seeing was of value.

The man who talked to me was the associate pastor of the church. From time to time, he would set up meetings for us to talk. I still didn't tell him everything I saw. I guess I was still a little bit afraid, but it was as if someone had taken a weight off my shoulders.

The next Friday night, during the concert at the church, an altar call was given, and I walked down to the front and gave my life to the Lord. So, for some time after that, I was what you would call "young and on fire for the Lord." I didn't really do things differently in my day-to-day life. It wasn't as if I had to stop drinking, smoking, or doing drugs, and I never used profanity much. About the biggest change in me was how I would talk about God and the Bible. These words had not been in my vocabulary before this transformation, but they most certainly were there now. I think people at my work noticed it the most, because they became tired of me talking about the latest verse that I had just read for the first time in my life. I wasn't able to stop talking about the word of God. This was all so new to me, and there were now people actually interested in what they called "seeing in the spirit." It seemed that I had a whole new vocabulary, and instead of calling them little entities or disfigured, burnt chimpanzees, I actually had a descriptive word that I could call them.

**

I saw demonic entities and found out that I actually had power over them. Now I finally understood why they responded the way they did to what I thought was my magic verse, Psalm 23. These demonic entities knew the word of God, and when it was being spoken in their presence, it had very little to do with me—but it had everything to do with the power of God's word. The Lord had granted me and any believer the right to bind them and/or cast them out in Jesus's name.

When I went home to my stepdad and mom's house, I shared my wonderful news with them. They thought I had gone a little nuts. I didn't share with them my newfound knowledge of angels and demonic entities, but I did share what I could, which was the word of God. I don't know if it was because of me, or if they had done it on their own, but just after that, my stepsister and my stepbrother both gave their lives to the Lord as well. So not only did I have godly men whom I could share what I saw in the spirit with, but I also had two family members whom I could share my faith with. It was an incredible time in my life, and spiritually speaking, I was moving in the right direction. There were still decisions to be made on my future. Would I stay in fast food, or maybe dare to go to college? I felt that in the Lord Jesus Christ, I could pretty much conquer anything.

Chapter 5

I finished my senior year of high school. In baseball, I became a designated hitter. It still hurt to throw the baseball, but I really did enjoy batting. And with the help of a new friend who spent most of his time on the bench I learned how to juggle baseballs with my one good arm. Not a lot of college scholarships are given for this talent, but I had learned to make lemonade from lemons. In football that year, and the year before, I made a name for myself, with my oversized shoulder pads and my ability to read an offense and cheat while seeing in the spiritual realm. I had given my life to the Lord, but some things were just worth exploiting. After all, I was human, not perfect.

The stronger I became, the more people began to take notice. Lifting weights had paid off, along with maintaining my quickness from being a receiver. This worked well for me. I was awarded first-team all-league and state mention, in the very competitive state of California. That wasn't bad for a skinny, little homeless kid. The way I saw it, I would never forget where I came from, because in Jesus's name I was never going back. I had come a long way from living in the janitor's closet at the high school, but I had every ounce of faith that God my father would never leave me or forsake me as my earthly father had. Whatever obstacles were before me, I could somehow, some way, overcome them. I knew my path had just begun. Who knows? Maybe I could become the first person in my family ever to go to college and get a degree.

I continued to work at the fast-food restaurant, where I had become a store manager. I enjoyed what I did and had been doing it for so many years I could just about do it in my sleep. I had fun with my staff, and most of them were about the same age I was, give or take a few years. In some ways, I fell away from my classmates I was about to graduate with and seemed to gravitate more toward my church family, my coworkers, and my stepbrother and stepsister.

***

After graduation from high school, I talked to the counselors at one of the local colleges. It was a large town, and there were several to choose from. My grade point average from high school was not going to wow anyone, but I enrolled in some classes as a part-time student to see if maybe I could pull out some type of miracle. In my case, my high school grades just followed me. I could keep up, but just barely. I was struggling again, and all I was working on was my prerequisites that I had failed to complete in high school. My counselors would assure me it would get easier as I went on. I think they just wanted to keep the enrollment numbers up. I finished my first year, but with part-time school and full-time work, I felt as if my head would explode.

***

The demonic entities weren't as common in college. I did think, from time to time, that some of my teachers were demonically possessed, but that was just me. It wasn't what I saw in the spirit, but just a feeling I had in my gut, more so because I was struggling so much. Instead of the demonic activity being a distraction to me, girls had taken front seat as far as my distraction went. I played some football on a very minimal scholarship, but I had been told that if I did not keep my grades up, that would go away. The game was easy; the grades were hard.

I had a part-time girlfriend; it was a bit of a joke because with being the manager of a fast-food restaurant, going to school part time, church, and the gym, I didn't have much time for personal relationships. We did go to church together, and most of the time we would go on dates afterward. She had a lot of friends, so I wasn't even really sure what our relationship status was. I think my desire to have a girlfriend seemed to make me spiritually blind. I never really saw anything demonic with her, but I sensed things. With everything I had going on in my life at that time, this relationship would have to take a backseat for now. I think the only thing that helped me go as far as I did in college was the fact that my stepbrother was incredibly intelligent and helped me with homework more often than I care to admit.

I believe some of my teachers thought I was bipolar, because in the classroom, I was generally asleep, but by some sort of miracle, my homework looked really good. In truth, I don't think I was fooling any of them, and I'm pretty sure the only reason I received the grades I did was because of my stepbrother's homework papers. If I could have, I would've had my stepbrother sitting for me in class with the other fifty students. There was only one problem with that solution: my stepbrother was five feet seven and about 140 pounds, and I was six feet tall and 215 pounds. Somehow, I think they would've noticed. There was also the fact that he would have known all the answers to most of the questions, and I was the guy falling asleep in the back of the room. What I found out was, I was still the same person I had been in high school. They say that the definition of insanity is doing things the same as you have always done them and expecting a different result.

***

I had a lot more peace in my heart due to my walk with God, but as for football, school, and work, they were about the same; I was just a whole lot happier about how I went about my life. Having people to talk to and share God's word and not keeping things all bottled up inside was still life changing. But I was going to have to make a decision about college. Everything else was going well, and as much as I wanted to be the first person in my family to go to college, it seemed that it was going to be much more difficult than I thought. About halfway through my second year, I called it quits. I had already been told that my partial scholarship would be dropped, and I would have to pay for my entire tuition if I was going to stay in school.

In some ways, it was a huge relief to walk away from the stress. I could focus more on church and Bible studies and continue my job as a fast-food manager. In my heart I knew that there were only a few more promotions I could receive in fast food. After that, I would have peaked in my career. They were already talking about moving me to a different store in a different town, and I really didn't want to leave my church family, my girlfriend, or my gym.

Shots Fired

One evening on my shift at work, we had already closed, and everyone was cleaning up their stations and doing the dishes. I was at my manager's desk, setting up my deposits for the next day and going over register tapes. My desk was located directly across the store from the drive-through window near the front counter, but out of sight from the people in the dining area. There were two safes, my desk with a small partition, and shelves above my head where we would keep condiments such as mayonnaise, mustard, ketchup, pickles, and so forth. As always, we were talking back and forth. Our staff got along very well, so they were laughing and joking with one another. At times I would have to tell them, "OK, that's enough. Let's get back to work."

As I stated before, usually while we were at work, I didn't see a lot in the spirit. However, on this night, I started to see demonic entities crawling into our workspace. At this point in time, I wasn't really sure what that meant, but as I noticed more of them, I yelled back to my staff and asked, "Is something going on back there?"

They just laughed and said, "Nothing that you need to know about."

So I just repeated my earlier statement and said, "Let's get things done. I want to go home."

This store was not in the greatest of neighborhoods, so taking into account the demonic entities that had entered my store, along with this particular neighborhood, what happened next probably should not have been a big surprise. In the blink of an eye, the butt of a gun was smashed through our drive-through window. My obvious reaction was to just look in that direction. Then the barrel was put into the window and began firing rounds throughout the store. Our building was made out of brick, so the bullets were just ricocheting around like bees in a hive. I yelled to my staff to get on the floor. I squatted down in my small space like a catcher in a baseball game and put my hands over my head. The shooter must have thought it was quite entertaining to shoot the condiment jars above my head, because all sorts of mustard, ketchup, and other condiments were pouring down on me and my desk. As the shooter drove away, I just sat on the floor and asked if everyone was OK.

One by one, they very cautiously came up to the front where I was sitting on the floor. Most of the bullets had hit around my general vicinity. I was still sitting on the floor with my hands over my head, splattered with an assortment of condiments. One of the girls walked toward me and giggled. She asked, "Are you OK?"

I replied, "Other than the fact that I hit my elbow on the safe, I think I'm OK."

She smiled and said, "You look like a mess" and with that she grabbed a towel and started to wipe me off. She looked at my right arm where I had thought I had hit my elbow, but what I thought was ketchup on my shirt and pants was blood. I had been shot in the lower part of my right tricep. They wrapped up my arm with gauze from the first-aid kit.

***

In that part of town, the police took their time getting there, and the paramedics would not show up unless the police were already on scene. The authorities were notified of the incident, and I called my supervisor to let him know what had happened. My staff wanted to start cleaning up the mess, but I told them to go in the dining room and sit until the police got there to look over everything before we cleaned up all the evidence. One of my staff members asked, "Are we getting paid for this? Because if we aren't, it's not worth it."

I said, "Yes, we are all still on the clock, so let's just sit and wait."

The girl who had bandaged my arm yelled at the young man and said, "You're worried about getting paid, and our manager just got shot!"

Minutes later, the police showed up, and the paramedics came shortly after that. The police walked around the store, took some pictures, and asked us all some questions. The paramedics asked if anyone was hurt, and of course all of my staff pointed at me and said, "Yeah! He got shot."

They rushed over to me, and I smiled and said, "I thought I hit my elbow on the concrete safe, but I guess I was wrong."

They took a look at my arm and determined that it was not a direct hit, but a ricochet. One of the paramedics said, "If you let me, I think I can see the bullet."

I said, "Why not?"

He took some long tweezers out of a sterilized wrapper and began to poke around in my arm and then announced, as if he were playing the game Operation, "I got it!"

He asked the police if they needed the bullet for evidence, and the police said, "No, I think we have enough ricochet bullets here for evidence. If they want that one as a souvenir, just let them have it."

So the paramedic dropped the bullet into my hand and began doing some first aid on my injured tricep. The girl who had first come to check on me and wrapped my arm asked me if she could keep it.

I asked, "Why in the world would you want this bullet that was in my arm?"

She said, "I want to make a necklace out of it."

I replied, "OK, but you better clean it up first."

She smiled and seemed to be so happy that I had given her my bullet. My supervisor had shown up by this time, and he asked me if I wanted to go home. I said, "No, I'm good. Let's get this mess cleaned up."

A couple of weeks later, the girl who had asked for the bullet came to work with a big smile on her face and gave me a hug. I said, "What was that for?"

She said, "For the necklace you gave me. Isn't it cool?" Hanging around her neck was a scratched-up and deformed bullet.

I just smiled and said, "You're welcome."

Learning My Authority

In my church I had been having regular meetings with the associate pastor. He was very interested and persistent in getting me up to speed concerning my authority in Jesus's name. One Sunday morning our church took members of the church in a bus to a nearby lake to baptize people. I was baptized in this lake with about a hundred other people. It was an incredible experience. When we came back to the church, my pastor friend shared with me two scriptures on my authority. One was Philippians 2:9 NLT: "Therefore God exalted him (Jesus) to the highest place and gave him the name that is above every name. The other was Luke 10:17 NLT: "…even the demons/devils obey us in your (Jesus') name." Because I was used to interacting with them anyway, I thought this would be interesting, trying out my new authority "in Jesus' name."

One evening my friend whose parents had taken me from the janitor's room came into the restaurant where I worked. I took a break to sit down and catch up on things he was doing. He asked me to come over to his parents' house to visit. So later that week, I went to his house to visit him and his family, just catching up on whatever was happening in their lives at that time. Later, my friend and I went up to his room, and when I saw the stairs going up to the attic room, I had a thought. If I had authority over these demonic entities, then I could tell them to leave in Jesus' name, and they would have no choice.

I asked my friend if I could go upstairs to my old room. He said, "Why do you want to go up there?"

I said, "No real reason. Just thought it would be fun to see it again."

He said, "As long as you don't ask me to come up there with you."

I replied, "I'll be back down in just a minute."

So I went up the stairs in hopes that the two demonic entities would be there. It was still daytime, so I don't know if that had anything to do with it, but I just walked around the room and didn't sense or see anything. I was so disappointed. I went back downstairs and continued to visit with my friend. I asked him if I could come back later that week, and he said, "Sure. That would be great."

***

For some time, my stepdad had been asking me what my extended plans were, since I wasn't in school and just worked at the fast-food restaurant. He had let me stay at our house while I was in college, but now that I was a college dropout, I would have to find my own place to live. He also inquired if I had thought any more about joining the military. To get him off my back, I said I would go down and talk to a recruiter. He said, "That's a great idea. I'll go with you."

Walking in with a master sergeant in uniform was the last thing I needed. My stepdad's opinion was that the only branch I should talk to was the air force.

Since I had struggled in the classroom, I believed I would be better suited for the army or marines, but that was never going to be an option with my stepdad. I had enjoyed working at the fast-food restaurant, but because it was my first real job and that was all I had ever known, I felt I needed to do something different. Maybe I would look at the military as a real option for my future.

***

The church that I was attending was still great. I felt I was learning so much about the word of God, as well as what the pastors would call my "gift." They also explained to me that a seer was someone who could from time to time see into the spirit realm or sometimes have dreams or visions. When I was younger, I thought that the demonic entities called me "seer" as my name, but in fact what they were doing was recognizing that I had a gift as a seer.

***

A friend of mine told me that where she worked was looking for part-time help, and they would train you to do the job as well. She worked in a nursing home as a CNA, or certified nursing assistant. It was just part time, and since I wasn't in school, I thought I would give it a try. My schedule at the fast-food restaurant allowed me to have days open for school purposes, so I only worked evenings. At this point, I had not made a decision about the military.

I started working at this nursing home three or four days a week in the mornings and at the fast-food restaurant at night. I was quickly certified as a CNA, and they wanted me to come on staff full time, but the money was better at the restaurant. While I was still working part time, they talked me into getting certified as a CMT, or certified medical technician. So in the mornings, I went to school for a number of weeks, and I was certified to pass out medications at the nursing home. I really liked what I was doing because I was able to help people, and it was a great change of pace from the fast-food restaurant. Also, it seemed there was a lot more angelic activity attached to the geriatric patients at the home.

Many of my coworkers at the nursing home were wonderful people, but as in most jobs, there were a few people who were there for the wrong reasons and seemed to be dealing with demonic spirits following them into the job place. I felt bold enough to approach them and try to get them to talk. Most would say it was none of my business, and how did I know those things anyway? But on occasion, people would listen and asked me if I would pray with them. I liked being at the nursing home, but I still wasn't sure if that was a career path that I wanted to stay on.

***

Sometime later, I decided to go back to my friend's house where I had lived when I was younger and try my luck again with the demons in the attic. On this visit, my friend wasn't there—just his mom and dad and sister. They enjoyed listening to me talk about church but had no intentions of actually going with me. I asked if I could go and visit my old room again. They found that odd but said it would be fine. I went upstairs, hoping to find the two demonic entities who had showed me the passageway in the wall that led down to the catacombs. It was nighttime, and I felt I would have better odds while it was dark. I was right. As I came to the top of the stairs, they were crouched in one corner of the room. I felt confident with my newfound knowledge. As one of them stood up, the other one stayed crouched.

I said to the one that was standing, "I come in the name of the Lord Jesus."

He stopped me and said, "Why?"

I said, "You need to leave this building in Jesus's name."

He looked at the one crouching and then looked back at me and said, "We will be back. We have been here for many years." At the time, I didn't really understand this.

I just knew I had the ability to cast them out, so I said, "In Jesus's name, you need to leave right now."

They seemed to move away, and then they were gone.

My friend had come home by then, and he yelled up the stairs, saying, "Please tell me that you are talking to yourself."

I just laughed and said, "Something like that."

When I came down, he said, "Why do you keep wanting to go up there?"

I said, "It's kind of a cool place. Have you ever been up there?"

He said, "Sure, about halfway up the stairs, and then my sister screamed, and I ran back down. For some reason, I've never been up there since. But the fact that you keep wanting to go up there makes me want to go too."

I said, "Let's go up there."

Of course, he said, "You go first."

So I did, and he followed only to the top of the stairs.

He said, "It's a little weird, but I can see why you like it."

I thought, "You would say that, now that we are in a demon-free zone."

He sat down on the top step. I went over to the mattress sitting on the floor, and we talked for a few minutes. After that he said, "OK, that's enough. Let's go back downstairs."

I told him there was nothing to be afraid of up here now, but I could see he didn't like this location in his house, so we went back downstairs. At a later date, I would come back to my friend's house, and yes, I would go upstairs just to see if the demons were still there. I never felt their presence there again.

***

I mentioned that the city was old, founded in 1870, but the Spanish had come much earlier, in 1774. So there were many old buildings that my friends and some establishments boasted to be haunted. I thought this sounded like fun—as was once said in a famous movie, "I ain't afraid of no ghost."

I felt pretty sure they were just demonic entities trying to create fear. They were beings I had already tried out my theory on, at my friend's house. I thought I would try another friend who worked at the fast-food restaurant. He lived in a very old house and said that he and his mom had not had a good night's sleep in this house since moving in. He claimed there was some sort of clunking noise every night, and they both claimed they could hear a voice from time to time. The dad slept like a rock and had no idea what they were talking about, but he did know they would not stay in the house alone at night. I asked him if I could come over at night and stay late to see what they were talking about. I was very curious.

I went over to his house after his mother and father had already gone to bed. His siblings had never lived at this house, so they thought they were crazy. Sure enough, very late that night, I heard a thump.

My friend said, "Did you hear that?"

I smiled and said, "Let's see where that's coming from."

He said, "How about I just stay here, and you go?"

I nodded my head and went on my quest. This was an old house like the one I had lived in with my friend. I don't really know how old, but it was two stories above ground, with a basement. At that moment, I was on the ground floor, and it sounded as if the thumping was coming from the second floor, so up the stairs I went. I have to admit I had some butterflies in my stomach. I was familiar with the entities in the attic where I had lived previously.

In my mind, this was like Peter stepping out of the boat in faith. On the second floor, I waited and listened for the thumping, and as my luck would have it, there was no thump. I just walked slowly. It was then that I saw a demonic entity. It looked at me, and I thought, "Same old, same old."

I don't know why, but I pointed at it with my finger to let it know I could see it.

It did something strange by manifesting into the form of a woman. I had not seen this before. She tried to say something to me that I did not understand.

I felt I had seen enough and decided it was time for me to end this. I said, "In Jesus's name, be gone."

It looked at me and just started moving away down the hall; I followed the entity and said it again. Very quietly, the entity just left.

I walked around to every room I could to see if the Lord would show me any more demonic entities. None were there, so I went downstairs and decided to go to the basement. Again I found nothing.

So I went back to my friend and said, "I'm pretty sure you're not going to hear that thumping noise or that lady's voice anymore."

He said, "I never told you it was a lady's voice. How would you know that?"

I said, "Because she is no longer here."

He was a little freaked out and didn't even want to know how I knew, or what I did.

Later, he told me that he didn't sleep very well that night. He said, "Really, I was just waiting to hear the thumping noise, and it never came." He said, "I don't know what you did, but it worked."

I said, "Come to church with me, and maybe I can explain it better."

He just smiled and said, "I don't think I'm ready for that yet."

I said, "When you are, let me know."

***

In my off time, when I wasn't at work or in the gym, I would try to find these houses that people would pay to go in and be scared, supposedly haunted by ghostly entities. My friends would agree to go with me, but I was not going to be scared. I was going to see if what these people claimed was a demonic entity or was just a fake.

My church friends weren't quite sure why I wanted to go to these so-called haunted houses. I would tell them "research." My work friends thought I was just crazy. I would say to them that I wanted to see just how real these haunted houses were. I thought it would be better to go to my first haunted house with people from church.

Again, I felt like Peter stepping out of the boat, with his friends in the boat thinking either "I wish I had his faith" or "My friend is a little crazy." Either way, from the minute we walked into this house, my two friends stayed right behind me. At least, unlike Peter's friends, they did stay with me, in very little faith.

I'm guessing this was one of those old buildings they had made up to be creepy. I never really sensed anything demonic about it. In fact, other than the fear that was displayed in their patrons, I sensed or saw nothing. So this first quest that I went on with my friends did not turn out to be all that I had hoped. I guess that even the best of hunters sometimes don't find the game they're looking for.

One of my friends' dads was the manager of an icehouse. They don't have those much anymore. One evening, they were getting rid of a whole truckload of dry ice. Some of my friends decided to load up the beds of their trucks with this dry ice. This meant only one thing. We were going to have some fun. We took the trucks into the old cemetery and drove around throwing out dry ice with shovels. It was sometime after midnight, and there was dew on the ground, just enough to make a nice fog throughout this cemetery. There were headstones dating back into the 1700s. Now, most of my friends from the restaurant were not Christians, so I'm sure that they brought some liquid refreshment to help them to be a little bolder. I, on the other hand, just wanted to see what would manifest at this early hour of the morning, in the dark, in fog, with fear running rampant.

We decided to break into two-person teams—obviously, one boy and one girl—and play hide-and-seek. I'm sure that some of the guys assumed there would be some making out, but it seemed to me that due to fear, most of the girls had no intention of this happening. We could hide only in the areas that had fog and could not go outside that, so luckily, it was not the entire cemetery, as it was extremely large.

I volunteered to be "it." The girl I was with protested, but I insisted it would be fun. So she informed me she was going to grab the back of my shirt and not let go. Needless to say, the back of my shirt was very stretched out by the end of night. I was counting on my ability to see in the spirit and on the fact that most of our group was terrified to be there, in order to be able to identify their locations through the manifestation of demonic spirits.

I was a young Christian and didn't really know how this worked. However, I thought, why not test the theory? As I dragged this poor, terrified young lady around the dark and foggy cemetery, two things became very apparent. Number one, it was hard to see anything, and number two, none of the demonic spirits that I was able to see had nothing to do with the people who were hiding. So much for my theory. We were able to find most of the couples, some because they just gave up and didn't want to be there. You would think it would be the girls, but in some cases, it was the guy. I could sense fear on them but was never able to see anything with them.

When I was a kid at my house, I saw things every day. Now, I seemed to see things only when God allowed them to manifest to me. Later on, I would talk to my pastor friend about this. He felt that God was shielding me from things I didn't really need to see.

***

Some of my friends and I decided to go check out one of these historically known houses that were said to be haunted. People actually made a pretty good living out of the manipulation of fear. It was in this house that I actually encountered demonic entities. If you could stay all night in this house, it was free to all members of your party. We were even assigned rooms to stay in for the night, and the next morning you would be refunded your money. The friends who went with me said if it wasn't too scary, they would stay the night.

There actually were demonic entities attached to this house, and after the first encounter, my friends felt that "Peter could walk on the water just fine by himself." So I did, and one by one, I was able to cast out many entities that night. The first and second entities appeared to me as a female adult and a female child. The adult tried to say something to me. I said, "Appear to me as your real self." My pastor friend had taught me to do this. At that time the entity who had tried to speak to me turned its head to one side and changed into the form that I was more familiar with—a singed, deformed, small, hairless chimpanzee. Then the one who had tried to speak to me said the one word that I had gotten accustomed to hearing: "seer." I proceeded to say in a low and calm voice, "In Jesus's name I bind you. You must leave in Jesus's name." I encountered other entities that night, and I repeated the same scenario each time.

I have to admit I didn't sleep very well. I often don't sleep well in beds I'm not familiar with, but at some point during the night, I did fall asleep. And when I woke up the next morning, the keepers of the house, who lived in a house across the street, came to greet me—and yes, refund my money. They said they would put my name on a plaque on the wall to let other people know that I had stayed the whole night.

I just told them it was a cool house, but the bed that I had slept in was not overly comfortable.

They laughed and said, "We don't get many guests to stay the whole night, so we will have to take your word for that."

Later, one of my friends and his parents went to this particular haunted house to take a tour, and according to my friend, there actually was a plaque with my name on it, saying that I was one of the few guests who had stayed an entire night. I thought that was kind of cool.

What I was finding out, in my own way, was that much of the time I could sense what was going on around me, but I was only able to see when God would allow me. This was actually a very good thing. As I said before, when I was a kid, there seemed to be no filter, and most of the time I saw things whether I wanted to or not, every minute of every day. Now, I was only allowed to see things that were relevant to a specific situation.

Chapter 6

After giving my life to the Lord, I would often go days and sometimes as much as a week without seeing in the spirit at all. This was very new to me, but I would come to realize it allowed me to focus on things with fewer distractions.

My girlfriend and I had always enjoyed going to church together as well as the usual stuff such as dinner and movies, or just hanging out at one of our houses and watching TV. We had known each other for quite some time, having met at the fast-food restaurant where I was the manager. My regional manager, who was also a friend of mine, said that as long as we kept the relationship quiet, he had no problem with it.

My girlfriend didn't really like the fact that I had talked to a recruiter about going into the military; she just wanted me to keep working at the fast-food restaurant and go to church events with her. But the military seemed the best option that I had. We had many discussions on how this might change our relationship. She had always viewed me as her supervisor from work. Even when we went on dates or church events, I was often the one who had to make decisions as to what we were going to do and when we were going to do it. I was OK with making decisions, but it was a role that I was forced into by the fast-food restaurant, and now by my girlfriend as well.

We talked about getting engaged before I went into the military, and her mom thought that was a wonderful idea. At the time, I wasn't really sure that I was ready, but often in my life I had done things because I was pushed into it. My girlfriend went back and forth on the whole engagement idea, sometimes saying that it would be a wonderful idea and other times feeling that she would miss her family too much, and her friends as well. So we decided to put the whole idea on the back burner and cross that bridge at a later date. This way, we could continue to work at the same restaurant where we had met.

Soon after that, a letter came from the restaurant upper management. If my girlfriend was going to stay working at this particular food establishment, she would have to move to a different restaurant. I called my district supervisor, who said that the word had gotten out that we were going to be engaged, and if she was going to keep working for this company, she would have to move to a nearby restaurant. At the time, I didn't think it was really going to be that big a deal, but within one week, she was transferred to a nearby restaurant under a new manager.

***

By this time, things were going pretty well. Unless I was to stay in the fast-food industry for the rest of my life, I needed to figure out some future plans. All I had ever known since I was a kid was fast food, and I really felt that it was time for a change in my life.

The air force was beginning to sound like a possible plan for my future. I had scored surprisingly high on my ASVAB, or armed services vocational aptitude battery. In civilian terms, it's the test you have to take to qualify for entry into the military. There was also a physical as well as a psychological test. It was 1981, and public opinion of the military was not good. Many people questioned why I would choose this direction. Well, my dad was a navy man, my stepdad was air force, and part of me needed a direction for my future. The other part of me was proud to serve my country. Many of my friends, coworkers and even my girlfriend would question my decision. Some even chose to not associate with me anymore. It was bad enough that I had become a Christian, and now this. This was Southern California, and they were entitled to their own opinions and feelings. I did have support from my stepbrother who was former Coast Guard, and of course my stepdad, who tried to prepare me for basic training and whatever else was to come.

***

Once I was accepted into the air force, I learned very fast that the military had a hurry-up-and-wait policy. I had a basic training date in the fall of 1982, so that gave me time to prepare myself physically. I had lifted weights for quite some time, but cardiovascular exercise was not something I enjoyed much. I would have to shift gears and learn to run. It wasn't as if it was foreign to me. I had played sports since I was a kid, and running was one of the common denominators, so I knew I could push myself to do this. At one point in time, I really enjoyed it, but I still like the results of lifting weights better.

I would, of course, miss being at my hometown church, as well as my girlfriend, whom I was becoming attached to. I felt not having the fellowship of my friends and pastor would be tough. My pastor assured me I would be fine, that God was with me wherever I went in the world. He said to trust that even when I was put in harm's way, God would still surround me with his hedge of protection, Psalm 91.

Most of the people around me on a daily basis had no idea what I was planning to do. I felt that I didn't need the criticism, so I did what I had learned to do best in life, which was to stay quiet. I would go on about my days, which were filled with church, my girlfriend, work, running, and lifting weights. By the time summer came in 1982, I had dropped down to 205 pounds. At six feet tall, even I thought I looked OK. My recruiter said that he had hoped I wouldn't stand out too much in basic training. He said it could put a target on my back for the TIs. In my mind, I thought the worst they could do to me would be to make me do push-ups or run. I did that for fun.

The one thing I had not anticipated was the spiritual aspect of basic training. My stepbrother or stepdad had very little to say about what I was to expect once I arrived in San Antonio, Texas. All I knew was God would never leave me nor forsake me.

***

Now that my decision had been made to go into the military, my girlfriend and I would have to make some type of decision as to what our future would be. It would be either to just stay in contact with each other and see if a long-distance relationship would work for us or to get engaged and possibly married after basic training and before my tech school started. Maybe we should just get married before I went to basic training.

Spiritually speaking, I felt as if we were moving far too fast to make any kind of lifetime decisions, but as always, the decision seemed to be left up to me. I knew that I needed someone in my life; I just wasn't completely sure that this was *the* someone I needed. But I also knew that I was going to be leaving for basic training in the fall, and once again there was a big decision to be made concerning my future. So to the delight of my girlfriend's mother, we decided to get married two weeks before I was to go to basic training. With that, I had made two life-changing decisions in a very short period of time.

***

I continued to work at the fast-food restaurant while preparing for basic training and my wedding. I did let most of my staff know that I would be leaving soon, so it wouldn't come as such a surprise. My now fiancé also continued to work in the fast-food restaurant that she had been moved to. As odd as it may seem, I was never able to see anything in the spirit concerning my fiancé. I wasn't really sure if it was because I didn't want to see or that I just wasn't able to. I did know that she continued to go back and forth when it came to moving away from her mom, sister, job, and the church that we had attended. I felt as if the only reason she said yes was because her mom wanted her to, and she had been put into a situation where she had to make a decision and yes seemed to be the correct answer.

In the last few weeks before I went to basic training, I decided to call it quits and stop working at the fast-food restaurant to give myself time to spend with my fiancé. We had not given ourselves much time to plan a wedding, which was going to be at my soon-to-be mother-in-law's house. The wedding was going to be performed by one of the pastors from our church. My fiancé's sister was to be her maid of honor, and my best man was my friend whom I had lived with after being homeless.

***

It all seemed like a blur, and before I knew it, we were married and had gone on a very short honeymoon. Since we weren't going to be reconnected until after basic training, she stayed at her mom's house for the time being. About five days before I was to go to basic training, I decided to surprise my new wife at her work. When I pulled into the parking lot, I ended up being the one who was surprised. In the back of the parking lot was my new wife and her manager. She had her back up against his car and he was leaning into her as they made out.

As my new wife looked up and noticed me sitting there in my car, she pushed him away and said, "It's not what you think."

Many things went through my mind, such as, How could I be able to see in the spirit and not notice this happening? Should I get out of the car and beat this guy into the ground, or should I just leave? Because if I got out of the car, I would probably get in trouble, and I really didn't need that before I went into the military.

I got out of the car and started making my way to my wife and her manager, but before I got there, he shoved her out of the way and climbed into his car from the passenger side. He proceeded to lock the doors and start the engine. I'm sure there were demonic entities by this time moving all over this parking lot, and if there were, I didn't notice one of them. All I knew was that this tall, skinny, red-headed guy who had just had his hands all over my wife was going to get his hind end kicked. She kept saying something like "I can explain," but I really didn't want to hear about it. So I took the side of my fist and started beating on top of his car until I was sure I had left a dent.

He really wanted to back out of his parking space, but my car was in the way, and customers had begun to gather around to see the potential fight. Realizing he wasn't going to get out of the car, I started walking back to my car to get in and leave. My wife kept saying over and over, "I can explain," but I guess I really wasn't in the mood to hear her explanation.

Later that day, she came by and told me that she had just wanted to see if there was anything between them.

I responded by saying, "Well, when I pulled up in the parking lot, it didn't look like there was anything between you, and as tight as you were holding each other, I'm pretty sure you couldn't have slid a newspaper in."

She said she had just wanted to see because he had been making advances toward her for a long time. I told her that I didn't really need this distraction right now, because soon I would be in basic training, and I didn't need to be wondering if my wife was making out with some guy just to find out if there was anything there or if she still liked me. She said, "It's really not like that."

In that moment, I realized that most of the women I had known in my life had caused some degree of pain. My real mom, after the divorce, didn't care to find out about my whereabouts after my dad had moved to the Midwest. My stepmom had kicked me out of the house and felt it was better that I live on the streets than with her and my dad. Now my wife, who in a matter of days was going to be left by herself for months. I had to wonder just how faithful to me she would be. Her mom was sick over the situation, but her sister supported her and said that we had just moved too fast. I'm sure she was right, but the fact was we were married, and in two days I was going away for almost two months.

***

On the night we were to leave to go to basic training, about twelve of us were housed in an old hotel in downtown LA. We were given strict orders not to leave the hotel. At this point of my life, I had not been in many hotels, and I was pretty sure none of us were going to get much sleep. Some of the new recruits had no idea what to expect when we got there. I felt pretty lucky because between my stepbrother and stepdad, they had prepared me extremely well.

    I wasn't really sure how I would respond academically, but I had no doubt that l physically stood out from my peers, and as my recruiter had said, it didn't go unnoticed. The consensus among my fellow recruits was that they were going to look like me by the end of basic training. I wasn't really sure how that was going to happen, since I had trained for years to look the way I did. Maybe they had some type of incredible training program to transform these guys, who looked as if they had never trained a day in their lives. These twelve recruits made a decision that night, for some reason, that they were going to follow me into basic training. I thought, "Well, here we go. The blind leading the blind."

That night, I used a pay phone in the hallway of the hotel to call my wife. I tried to figure out what her thoughts were for the direction we were going to take. She seemed to be very sorry about what had happened. She said they were going over to the restaurant where I used to be the manager to borrow some paper goods. This was something that we did in the restaurant chain often. She said that he started to open the door for her, but instead of opening the door, he put both hands on the roof of his car and started kissing on her. She said she didn't know why, but she responded to it, and that was when I pulled up. Then she continued to say that she was sorry and it would never happen again.

I really wanted to forgive her. It also helped me to clear my mind and have some sense of peace. She said she would write me letters while I was in basic training as often as she could. I told her that it sounded good and that I would do the same. Whenever they would let me, I would try to call her on the phone. In truth, I was just trying to get my mind prepared for what was about to happen in the days to come. Discussing my fears with my new wife was not going to help me at all in the weeks to come.

Basic Military Training (BMT)

Early the next morning, we were all awakened by someone banging on the doors saying, "Get up; get up; let's go." And it began. We grabbed what little we had brought with us and lined up in the hallway. They took a quick roll call, and out to the bus we went. It was so quiet on the bus that you could hear a pin drop, and even though I wasn't seeing anything in the spirit, I could sense fear was all around us.

When we arrived at LA International Airport, they shuffled us in, and we boarded the airplane. Now, I didn't come from much money, so this was the first airplane ride I had ever been on in my life. As I looked around, this seemed to be a first for almost everyone I was traveling with. In the spirit, all I could sense once again was fear, a presence that I was so accustomed to. However, this entity of fear was on me as well—fear of the unknown, and, in some ways, of what we had just gotten ourselves into.

***

With all the yelling going on by the people in uniforms, I almost felt right at home, like when I was a kid. So after we landed somewhere in Texas, we boarded another bus. It was a blue military bus. It was easy to tell who we were because we were all in civilian clothes, and everyone else on the bus was in a military green uniform. When we arrived at the base and shuffled off the bus, there were other recruits already there being yelled at, standing in rows in their civilian clothes.

Again, fear was abundant. I wasn't about to say anything, but some of the people yelling at us— I suppose they were TIs (Training Instructors)—had demonic spirits with them as well. I thought, "Should I try to cast these demons out or just leave them alone?" After all, God had showed them to me for a reason. In my own fear, I stayed quiet and did what I was told. As my recruiter had said, I was going to attract attention. Well, he was right. The first TI who came up to me was about five feet seven, and he yelled something to the effect of "I'll bet you think you can whip me. And where are you from, boy?"

I said, "Southern California."

He yelled something that I was going to hear over and over for most of basic training. "There's only two things that come from California: steers and queers. And I don't see no horns on you, boy."

There were a lot of things going through the minds of the recruits around me, but I'm sure they were not the same thing that was going through my mind, which was "Sir, if you want your wife to come back to you, we can bind those demonic spirits and set you free from that demon of deception that is standing with you."

Of course, I didn't say a thing. I was standing out enough, although in my young Christian mind, I felt that maybe I had been sent there to help some of these people. Maybe God would open the door and allow me to do some ministry, but now was not the time. For the time being, it seemed that any anger or ill feelings these TIs had was going to be dumped on the new recruits.

We were split up into flights. Our TI was about six feet tall and not quite as loud as the other TIs. He was a Technical sergeant, E-6. We also had a team leader, and he yelled quite a bit. He was a Staff sergeant, E-5. Our TI hung back a little bit and let the team leader do all the yelling. The good part was that the shorter TI, who had yelled at me earlier, would be our sister flight's TI. I felt lucky not to have to deal with him.

They lined us up and ushered us into a large building elevated on poles. We went up the stairs single file and into what would be our home for the next six weeks. They made me lead the line, so I was the first one into the building. They had us stand in front of lockers, and since I was first in the room, that put me all the way in the back corner. There were twenty-five guys per side with a semiwall down the middle, but it was open at the back and at the front of the building. Each of us put his personal belongings down in front of his locker.

They immediately shuffled us back downstairs onto a large concrete slab that was located underneath the dorm. We formed up, and they marched us over to get our haircuts and to be issued all the gear that we would wear for the next six weeks. Haircuts were interesting because some of the guys thought it was a good idea to get their hair cut short before coming. I, on the other hand, did not get my hair cut before coming. Being a kid from Southern California, I wore my hair about halfway to my shoulders, and the barber enjoyed cutting it down the middle, leaving the sides long, and then having a conversation with the barber next to him. At least I gave everyone something to smile about until he finished the job, and then I looked just like everyone else.

***

We went back to our building and put our new wardrobe into our lockers. They took all our personal belongings and locked them in a large closet. That first night, our TI and team leader both spent the night in a room that was located to the front of the bay with doors leading to each side of the building. I supposed this was to keep an eye on everyone. From the sounds of things that night, most of the recruits didn't get much sleep, and to be honest, I'm sure I heard one or two of them crying in low tones.

There was, without question, spiritual movement within this building, and I thought without a doubt that I could help the situation. Still, I stayed quiet. I'm pretty sure there were a lot of prayers said that night. Sometimes God puts us in situations where the only place we can look is up toward him.

The next day we were awakened by the sound of reveille. We were to fall out on the concrete pad located under the building in only our socks, T-shirts, and underwear. They called out one of the recruits by name, and he stepped out of the ranks and came to the front. It turned out that he was a thirty-year-old recruit who was going to be Air Force Reserve. He had a receding hairline but was in fairly good shape. He had a chest thick with hair, and because of his age, he was going to be our dorm chief.

They had us drop to the deck and pull our T-shirts over our heads so that we could not see anything. We got into a push-up position. The TI

said, "On my count we are going to do push-ups."
He would say, "Down, up," and the recruits would
say, "One." The TI would say, "Down, up," and the
recruits would say, "Two." And so on. I knew I
could do push-ups for days, so when we got to near
a hundred, all I knew was the TI's voice was
extremely close to my location, possibly even
sitting on the floor next to me. Now what you have
to understand is, even though the recruits had
stopped doing push-ups, they still had to count, so
as far as I was concerned, we were all still doing
push-ups.

At that point, the TI tapped me on the back
of the head and said, "Boy, we're all getting real
tired watching you do push-ups." It seemed that
most everyone else had dropped off in a relatively
short period of time. For quite a while, I had been
doing push-ups by myself. The TI said, "Looks like
we found our PT"—physical training—"monitor."
From that moment on, I would lead the flight in
calisthenics, flight runs, and anything else that had
to do with physical training.

***

It seemed that everyone in the flight (all fifty
recruits) had to have a job, all the way from
bathroom crew to the squad leaders and dorm chief.
They also asked if anyone had any experience with

making schedules. My fast-food management experience came in handy. I reluctantly raised my hand.

The TI said, "You're already the PT monitor; anyone else?"

They all just looked at one another, so the TI said, "I guess you'll have two jobs."

From then on, I was dorm guard monitor as well. As dorm guard, I had to have someone posted at the door twenty-four hours a day. The nice thing about making the schedule was that I never had to pull dorm guard duty in the middle of the night, so I always slept well.

At about the fourth or fifth day, some of the recruits were having a hard time adjusting. That night I went to the TI's office. He told me to come in and asked me what it was that I wanted. I asked if it would be OK if I could pray over the flight. My TI and team leader just looked at me. Finally, one of them said, "You want to pray over the flight?" They looked at one another and said, "Have you ever heard of anything like that?"

I said, "It's OK if I can't."

They said, "No, I want to hear this."

They both followed me out of the TI's room and into the bay. We were all getting ready to hit the rack, and I walked through each bay and asked each recruit if he had anything specific he wanted me to pray about. At first they didn't say much, but then it seemed they all had something they wanted me to pray about. I wrote it down on a tablet and went to the end of the bay between the two sections and began to pray. I even prayed over the TI and our team leader.

The next morning our TI said, "I have never seen anything like that, and if you want to, you're welcome to do it every night."

So I did.

***

That next morning after we did our calisthenics and ate breakfast, they said if we wanted to write letters to anyone back home or make phone calls, they were going to give us time to do that. For whatever reason, my flight insisted that I go first on the phones. There were about ten of them, and so I sat down and called my wife. Her mom said that she wasn't home and said she was sure that she would be sorry she missed my call. So I hung up the phone and called my mom and stepdad. We had a nice, short conversation, and I told them briefly about what was going on. I told them to give everybody back home a big hug and I would be talking to them soon.

The next day we went to get our dog tags. That seems simple enough, but they give you an option to put whatever your religious preference is.

When I said my religious preference was Christian, they said, "No, like Protestant, Methodist, Presbyterian, Catholic, and so on." They asked, "Which one are you?"

I said, "None of those. I'm a Christian."

At some point my TI came over and asked what the problem was. The guy making the dog tag said, "He wants me to put, as his religious preference, Christian."

My TI said, "So put Christian."

The man said, "We don't have that one."

My TI said, "Fine. Then we'll wait until you do."

My TI looked at me and winked with a little grin and said, "If the boy wants Christian, then I think it should be Christian." So we waited until the man could make a stamp that said Christian. To this day, my dog tags say Christian.

***

After about the first week of basic training, I went from sensing things around me to seeing in the spirit again. Being given permission to pray over our flight seemed to make a world of difference. I didn't know it before then, but I would start seeing more and more things with our staff sergeant team leader. One day we had a cleaning day in the dorm, which meant stripping the floors and doing a top-to-bottom clean. As I walked past the TI's room, I noticed our team leader sitting there with his head on his desk and his hands over his head. I had seen, from time to time, a demonic spirit with him, but I wasn't really sure how to interpret it.

I stopped at his door and asked him for permission to speak. He just looked at me and said, "Why not?" I asked him if he would mind if I shared something with him. He replied again, "Why not?"

Instead of telling him that he had a demonic spirit with him, I said, "I feel like you're having problems with your family, maybe your wife, and there seems to be an extreme weight on you, one that you can no longer carry around."

I said, "If you'll allow me to, I might be able to help."

His reply was "Why not, preacher boy? Have at it."

So I prayed for him, his wife and kids, and other things. After I said amen, I looked at him and knew he was trying to fight back the tears. He said, "Thanks." And then, "Go get some work done." (TIs seem to have a higher divorce rate than anyone else in the military).

The next day, I noticed that it was just our TI in the room up front. I stopped at the door and asked for permission to speak. He said, "What's on your mind?" I asked if our team leader was OK.

He looked at me and said, "I don't know what you said to him, but he thinks he needs to take some leave and spend some time with his wife and family, so he won't be here for a few weeks." He said, "Do you have any words for me?"

I don't know why I let the words come out of my mouth, but it was like I had no choice.

I said, "Your wife forgives you, and your kids really do want to reconnect with you."

He just shook his head and said, "How would you know anything about my wife and kids?"

I said, "I don't, but God does."

He just looked at me, and said, "Go back and help your boys."

I felt it was odd, but I was the only one in my flight, other than our dorm chief, who ever went into the TI's room. For some reason, I seemed to be in there all the time, and the rest of the guys in the flight were terrified to even walk past the door. I have to admit, I had a completely different relationship with my TI and team leader than anyone else in the flight. I had no question that it was just the favor of God surrounding me. Don't misunderstand me. Basic training was extremely tough. I think for each and every individual, it's different. For me, the physical aspect of it was easy. There is also a mental aspect where they try to get into your head and mess with you. The only real struggle I had was, as always, in the classrooms. I have no doubt some people would say that was the easiest part.

***

Every Sunday, they would allow us to go to chapel. This was the military version of church, and you could choose from different services. The TIs were never at chapel, and when we first started going to these services on Sunday, most of the troops wanted to go, if for no other reason than to get away from the dorm. The military members who spoke at chapel were called chaplains; they were always very nice to all the recruits. In the church that I went to at home, people were friendly, and the message that was given always spoke to me. We would also sing praise and worship music. I could just feel the spirit of God, and I loved it. I didn't ever remember being bored in church. In chapel on the base, most of the people in attendance seemed to be scared to death, probably because we were in basic military training. The message that was given by the chaplain was usually just him reading out of the Bible. This was good, but I think most of the recruits did not really relate to it well. All that I could sense in the spirit was just a type of sterile feeling, as if nothing was moving at all. When we sang, it was from hymnals. I had never really sung hymns out of a book, and for me and most of the people in chapel, it seemed to be very boring. In fact, most of the troops would use this time to get extra sleep, and we would have to wake them up when it was time to go. Eventually, fewer and fewer of the guys in our flight went to chapel with me. I continued because I felt that was what I was supposed to do.

I also liked Sunday because on the way back from chapel, I could stop at this large building that had about fifty phones in it. There were also little booths and chairs, so you were comfortable while you were talking on the phone. I would always call my wife first, and if she wasn't there, I would call one of my other family members, just to hear their voice. Throughout basic training, when I was able to reach my wife on the phone, she always sounded very upbeat and absolutely sure about our future.

***

When the flight was going somewhere on base, we would line up and march in formation. There would be four rows of airmen, with four squad leaders in front, the dorm chief, and someone carrying the flight's flag. On one weekend, we were forming up to go eat dinner at the chow hall. After marching, the flight would stop in front of the dining facility, and the chow runner (that was a person's job from our flight) would run up and stand in front of the door to the chow hall. There was a window in the door, and the chow runner would look in the window, and when there was enough room for the flight to get in line, he would open the door and call the flight into the chow hall. Unfortunately, our TI had a sense of humor, and our chow runner was too short to look in the window. He had to jump up a short distance and peek in, standing at attention while doing this. Obviously, if you're jumping up and down, you're not at attention.

On the weekends, sometimes the TIs would be with us, and sometimes not. On this particular weekend, he was not with us. Our flight was in line, waiting for our chow runner to let us into the chow hall. Our sister flight, with the short, angry TI, was also in line to go to the chow hall. I don't know why he picked this particular day—maybe because our TI was not with us—but it made him angry that our chow runner had to jump to see in the window, so he quickly walked up behind our flight's chow runner and said something to him. We weren't sure what he said, but our chow runner was afraid to jump after that, so he couldn't see in the window to let us know if it was clear for us to go in.

Keep in mind that this was in 1982. The drill instructors or TIs had all the right in the world to put their hands on you for pretty much any reason. He began to yell into our chow runner's ear loud enough that we could all hear. He said, "What are you going to do? And whatever it is, I don't want to see you not standing at attention."

Without our TI there, you would have thought our dorm chief would have done something, but no, he did nothing. I am one of those people who can take only so much, and then something is going to happen. So I stepped out of ranks and walked up to the chow runner, who was shorter than this short TI. I was trying to keep as much military bearing as possible, and I said to our chow runner, "Go back to the ranks. I will take your position."

I didn't have to tell our chow runner twice, so he stepped out and double-timed it back into the ranks. I could easily see in the window. I thought that was using some ingenuity on my part.

But our sister flight's TI didn't like that one little bit, so he shoved me to one side and said, "You think you're smart, don't you boy?"

I went back to the window and stood at attention. I could see him out of my peripheral vision, and when he took his TI hat off and laid it on the ground, I thought I might be in trouble.

Thinking fast, I said, "TI, I need to open the door so I can let my flight in to eat chow."

He shoved me with one hand and said, "Not until we go round and round."

The next thing I knew, he shoved me and said, "Come on."

Now, I knew that he wasn't allowed to throw a punch at me, so I figured this was just going to be a wrestling match. I also knew that I was quite a bit stronger than he was, so when he ran at me, I had flashbacks of being a linebacker in high school and college, and before he could take two steps, I picked him up off the ground and drove him into the concrete slab. He let out a yell, and I was bound and determined not to let him up. I looked over at the rest of my flight, and they were all shuffling to get a good view of what was going on.

As if he were a guardian angel, I saw my TI, and he had a big smile on his face. He walked up to us and said, "Boy, let that man up."

As I got up, he grabbed the short TI by the arm and said, "Don't be messing with my flight."

The only words our sister flight's TI said were "Tell him to give me a 341." Every airman had three pieces of paper in his pocket, called a form 341. They used them for disciplinary actions.

Our TI said in a quiet voice, "I'd like to see you take one from him."

Our sister flight's TI picked up his hat off the ground, dusted some loose gravel off his uniform, and walked back to his flight. He yelled at his dorm chief and said, "Get them in the chow hall." And then he walked away.

Our TI told the chow runner to get back to the door and get his flight into the chow hall and get them eating.

On weekends we generally got more time to eat because there weren't as many TIs. If the TIs ate in the chow hall, they sat at a group of tables that was known as "the snake pit." That day, our TI went in with us to eat, and there were only one or two other drill instructors in the snake pit. So he walked over to the table I was sitting at and sat down. This doesn't sound like a big deal, but when I went to basic training, that just didn't happen. Again, I have no doubt that throughout this entire situation, the favor of God was all around me.

My drill instructor said, "I'm proud of you, son. You're going to make one heck of an airman."

***

By this point, the guys in my flight were used to coming to me and asking me to pray with them, especially when they didn't want me to pray it out at night before they went to bed. Some things were just private. It was usually a prayer about a girlfriend or a wife, and sometimes it was about a sick family member, or maybe something that they were dealing with. This made me feel I had an actual God purpose in this flight and that I was there for a reason.

There was a struggle taking place within our flight, and it was something that I was unfamiliar with—a struggle that was usually at the center of my prayers at the end of the day. When I was growing up in Southern California during the sixties and seventies, prejudice was a word that I knew but didn't really understand. Growing up, I had friends who were all colors, religions, and nationalities. I was unable to relate to the word *prejudice* on a personal level. I lived a somewhat sheltered life on the street I grew up on. There were Asians, Hispanics, American Indians, and African Americans as well as Caucasians. I was never told there was a difference because of your skin color, but after going to basic military training, I found out that I had been taught much differently from the majority of the rest of our country. I don't know if they did it on purpose, to see how we would react, but the majority of our flight was made up of "good old Southern boys." I think just as a joke, they threw in a dozen Southern California boys just to make it funny.

But I noticed demons of deception constantly trying to stir the pot and disrupting the unity of our flight. Racial slurs were commonly used from both sides. Most of the time, I felt like the man in the middle, but in truth, I didn't understand the whole thing. I had been taught that we all bleed red and that Jesus died for us all. It didn't matter the color of your skin, whether you were tall or short, fat or thin. My dad taught me that we were all Americans, and in my mind and in our flight, that made us brothers. But I had been a part of the family long enough to know that brothers and sisters sometimes fight even though they love one another and would no doubt stand up and fight for one another. I would remind them that even though we didn't see eye to eye, we were brothers, and at the end of the day, brothers forgive one another. Someday we might have to fight together side by side, and at that point, the color of our skin would be absolutely irrelevant. No one in our flight would argue with me on this point. First of all, I had the title of BBOC (big boy on campus). Second of all, I seemed to be most everyone's friend, and in one way or another, they all trusted me. Once again, God's presence followed me.

***

One of the physical tests that we had to pass was the obstacle course. I'm pretty sure that this course has changed several times over the years, but it was tough, even for me, and I was pretty sure I was ready for most anything they could throw at me, physically speaking. I was told that at the time I ran this particular obstacle course, I set a new course record. All I knew was that I was ready for this, and as I crossed the finish line and looked back, I saw no one.

When your flight is running the obstacle course, it is just your flight, so I asked our drill instructor if I could run back and help the guys at the end. He in turn asked one of the course overseers if that was legal.

He just said, "Go!"

So I went. Luckily, there was a path down the side of the obstacle course. I went back as far as I could and then backtracked till I found our troop who was pulling up the rear of the flight. Really, all I did was cheer him on until he got to the barrel hill. This hill was made out of fifty-gallon drums. I don't really remember how tall it was, but it was pretty big, and at the top they had welded on vertical sidebars, and also a bar in the middle, with a long bar going all the way over the top. Once you reached the summit of the barrels, you had to crawl under this long bar.

This last troop was an Asian kid who had come with us from California. He was a bit on the short side and a little overweight, so to help him I pushed from the bottom of his boots and basically pushed him up the hill. Once he made it to the top, he swung his legs around to the other side, and gravity did the rest.

I stayed right with him until we got to the finish line. The rest of the flight was cheering us on.

This was a day that I would remember because after we had crossed the finish line, I yelled, "There is no north and south today—just a bunch of brothers in matching green outfits."

When we could finally put our differences aside, we found out we could do some pretty incredible things, such as winning honor flight, which our sister flight protested to the very end. I guess we made the little drill instructor mad, which made it feel that much better.

That night our TI did something that I guess was unheard of. He came to the door of our building with a dolly loaded down with a bunch of pizza boxes. He was in civilian clothes and knocked on our door. I was the dorm guard monitor, but I was not on dorm guard that night, and the dorm guard said his usual line: "Dorm guard, dorm A3. How can I help you?"

At that, the person at the door was supposed to show the dorm guard his ID card. You have to remember, to get to our dorm, you have to go up a flight of stairs, so our TI had just come up a flight of stairs with this dolly and a whole bunch of pizza boxes. He said, "I think I left my ID in the car, so just let me in."

The dorm guard on duty thought it was a trick and would not open the door. After a minute or two, the TI told the dorm guard to go get the dorm guard monitor, so I came back to the door with the dorm guard monitor. Our TI said the same thing again—about leaving his ID in the car. He just looked at me as if to say, "Please let me in."

So I relieved the dorm guard of his duty and opened the door. As the TI came in the door with the boxes of pizza, he said, "I trained you guys way too good. Grab a couple of guys and go downstairs and get the rest of the pizzas. There's also a cooler of sodas."

So we did just that, and that night we had a pizza party with our drill instructor and our team leader. They even asked me if I would bless the food. It was pretty incredible.

***

This all took place toward the end of our time in basic training. In the days to follow, we took our classroom portion of the testing procedures, and yes, I failed the first test. But after cramming that night and a lot of prayer, I was able to pass the written portion the following day. Some things never change.

The last thing I remember about going to basic military training school was our drill instructor and team leader marching us out to the parade grounds. It was there that he put us in parade rest (which means we were not standing at attention).

He addressed us not as a flight of recruits, but as a unit of airmen. He said, "It has been brought to my attention by one of your fellow airmen that I have neglected my family far too long, and with that, I will put in my paperwork to retire from the US Air Force and step down as a basic military training TI, handing off my next flight to my team leader. I find it only fitting that this flight, 3702, would be my last basic military training flight, and although I have had, over the years, many great flights, I must admit that I have never had a group of recruits that affected me the way this one has. As much as I have tried to teach you, I think that I may have been the one who learned something here. When you go on from here, remember the things that I have taught you, as well as the things your brothers have taught you, which may take you further in life.

"I learned that God comes before country, and I will continue to pursue that. I've always served my country before God, and I feel it's time to turn that around, as one of your fellow airmen is so fond of saying. 'God bless each and every one of you, and may He always keep you'.

***

We would all go our separate ways in the days to come. It was now time to go to our training schools

171

and to learn the jobs that we were going to perform in the United States military. For me, I was off to a training base in Illinois, in November, in the snow.

Divided but Not Conquered

I am not sure that I had ever seen it snow before in my life. That was about to change, because when we arrived at our training facility, there was about two feet of snow. What do you do in the military with two feet of snow? There is no such thing as a snow day. You get a whole bunch of airmen and hand them shovels. Until that job is done, you're going to keep shoveling. Obviously for me, shoveling snow was pretty new, but the truth was, I enjoyed the physical activity and considered it a new and cold workout. We were the new guys at the training school, and for us, classes hadn't started yet, so they used us for all sorts of oddball activities, such as kitchen duty, cleaning the dorms, and shoveling snow. I guess every rotation of airmen trainees had to take its turn in the in-processing system. For me, it was OK, because the thought of being in the training school was intimidating—it was all classroom work, and in case you just started reading this, classroom work was not my strong point.

***

Directly across the street from my dorm was a large call center building where, once again, there were about fifty phones with booths and chairs. So as soon as I could, I called my wife and told her about the piles of snow that we had to shovel, and as soon as I could get the paperwork through, they would allow her to come. We would stay in the military base housing that was set aside for military and their dependents. Her mom came on the phone and said that playing in the snow sounded like fun! I told her to make sure she brought plenty of warm clothes; I was sure she didn't own many.

There were a handful of airmen who came with me from my flight in basic training, and for the most part, we stayed together. We were given a little more freedom in tech school than we had had in basic training, so the idea of going to the chapel on Sundays was going to be a tough sell.

On Friday and Saturday nights, my friends wanted to go to the airmen's club (that means a bar that is on base), drink beer, and hang out. A lot of the time, I would go with them as a kind of designated driver. It sounds funny, but I was a big enough guy that most people wouldn't make fun of me for drinking a diet Shirley Temple, my drink of choice.

They always wanted to go off base to see if they could meet some girls out on the town, but in

1982 there were quite a few establishments with signs in the windows that read "No Dogs and No Airmen Allowed." And with the hairstyles in the early 1980s, it was very easy to tell if you were military, so we didn't fit in very well. In basic training, I had been introduced to a type of prejudice that I was unfamiliar with and thought I had seen firsthand what this was all about. But now, I found out that in the civilian world, sometimes it had nothing to do with the color of your skin. Sometimes it had to do with your haircut, which marked you as US military members. I felt as if we were training to fight for a country that didn't really want us at all. As a kid, I was different because of the things I was able to see and couldn't control. Now, as a young man, I realized I was being looked down upon because I had made the choice to serve my country in the military.

Most of the time we stayed on base, mainly because we were more accepted. Since we had no way to get around other than walking, it was the most convenient. On base I had my training school, the base chapel, and my all-important weight room. I was finally able to train in the weight room as much as I wanted to. Except for the school part, the training facility was incredible. The weight room on the military base was one of the best facilities I had ever been in. Unfortunately, I was there to go to school and learn the job I was to perform once I was assigned to an active-duty base. I felt I had to study much harder to pass the test than most other airmen, and as much as I wanted to work out in the weight room all evening, I had to make time to study for tests.

So, on the first Saturday that I was able to, I went into town and buy some free weights for my dorm room so that I could study and not have to leave my room to get my work out in. As my luck would have it, it started to snow as I was walking off base. I honestly didn't care, because I was on a mission. Now, on the weekends, we didn't have to wear our military uniforms. We did have some civilian clothes, and I had a stocking cap that covered my ears, so due to the amount of nonmilitary clothes I had on, I fit in downtown.

When I walked up to the sporting goods store in town, it had a sign in the window that read No Airmen Allowed, so I said a little prayer and walked in the door. I didn't dare take my stocking cap off. The man in the store asked me if there was anything he could help me with. I said I needed a set of standard free weights, so he showed me a few different sets of weights, and I picked out a basic 110-pound set. I wondered why this business owner would have a sign outside his store stating that he didn't want any airmen to shop there. I had money. I guess he had his own reasons, and I would never know what they were.

He brought me up a box from the back on a cart. It had a six-foot straight bar, one set of dumbbell handles, and 110 pounds of plate weight. He looked out of the front windows of his store and noticed there was no car. He said, "Did you walk here?"

I said, "Yes sir."

He looked at me and stared. It felt as if he stared for a couple minutes, but I'm sure it was only for a few seconds. At that moment, I wasn't really sure he was going to sell me the weights. I know it doesn't sound like it, but for me the presence of God was there, and so he rang up the purchase and said, "I hope you don't have very far to go, because it's coming down pretty good out there."

I walked out the door with a box of weights on my shoulder and a long bar in my other hand. By the time I reached the base and my dorm, there was snow piled up on my box. I'm sure I looked pretty funny walking up, and some of my fellow airmen who knew what I was doing yelled from their windows, "Look, it's Conan the Barbarian." I was just happy to have my weights in my dorm room. God is good.

***

The one thing that was tough about being in the military for me to this point was not really being able to read my Bible like I wanted to. I would rely on the base chapel to hear the word of God. The base chapel was a lot like the base chapel I had just come from—a somewhat sterile environment. I never really felt like I did in my church at home, but the Bible says that the word cannot go out and come back void, so I felt that as long as I was hearing the Bible being read, for now that would have to do.

I spent a lot of time in my training school by myself, making phone calls talking to my wife and sometimes my family, studying, lifting weights, and going to chapel. That was pretty much my day, unless, of course, the boys were going out on Friday or Saturday night. I have to admit, it started to get a little boring, babysitting drunk guys. I had been in this situation far too much as a kid, and it started being much more productive to just stay home and study.

So I found myself once again with not very many actual friends. My wife and family had sent me many letters while I was in basic training, so from time to time, I would get them out and read them. In some ways, it made me feel as if they were there with me. As always, when people needed prayer for something, I seemed to be the person they found. Usually, it had something to do with a girlfriend or fiancé back home. Either way, I was always happy that they came to me.

By the time we were about a third of the way through tech school, I finally received paperwork that approved me for joint spouse housing, which meant my wife could fly back and live with me in a base housing unit. As soon as I was able to, I called her on the phone and told her that I had great news; the paperwork had been approved for her to come back and join me on base. She seemed very excited, and we talked for quite some time about her coming out with me and the places we would go and see together. I told her that some of the guys I had talked about on the phone and in letters were here, and she would get to meet them. She asked me how the churches were on base, and I told her they were nothing like home, but we could make the best of it. We even talked about her driving my car back with her sister so that we would have something to drive while she was here, and her sister would visit for a short time and then fly back to California.

All the plans seemed very exciting. I have to admit I was looking forward to seeing her and thought this whole thing might just work out fine. I remember being on the phone that day for quite some time, and after being on the phone for about forty-five minutes and discussing everything that we were going to do, something changed. I could sense it in the spirit, but in truth, I didn't know what it was. We were talking and everything was great, but I sensed there was something that I didn't know. I said to her, "Is everything OK? If I need to let you go because you have things you need to do, that's fine. We can talk about this more later."

Her voice changed, and she said, "I didn't know how to tell you this, so I guess I'm just going to say it."

I could hear her mom in the background saying something like "Just tell him" and my wife saying, "I am! My mom and I went to the courthouse a couple of days ago and got our marriage annulled. I'm so sorry. I should've told you at the beginning of our conversation. The paperwork is in the mail, and when you get it, you don't have to sign it and send it back, because they said that wasn't necessary since we had not been married long enough."

I sat there in that call center desperately wanting to throw up. I said nothing.

She said, "Are you OK?"

Again I said nothing.

She said, "If you're still there, say something to me."

I said, "Why did you make me feel like everything was great? Why didn't you just tell me?"

She said, "It sounded like you were doing so great, and I didn't want to mess you up."

I said, "Is there someone else, or is it just the fact that you don't want to be with me anymore?"

She said, "Yes, there is someone else, and in truth we are thinking about joining the marines at the same time—so we can go to boot camp, training school, and be assigned to the same base later on."

I said, "So right now, at this moment, you are not my wife. Is that right?"

She said, "Yes, that is right."

I said, "OK then, I will let you go so that you can get on with the rest of your life. Give your mom a hug for me and tell her that I'm so sorry."

With that, she started to cry and said, "Why do you always have to make things so difficult?"

I never really answered that question. All I said was "Goodbye."

On the other end of the phone line, she said, "Please don't hang up yet! Please don't hang up!"

But I did hang up.

In a couple of days, an envelope came in the mail for me. It would be the last mail that I ever received from her, and as she had said, my marriage had been annulled by the State of California.

I was numb and had to explain to the military why I no longer needed to be in joint spouse housing. They told me that this sort of thing happened more than you would think and that they would take care of the additional paperwork to cancel the housing order. They also told me that it might be a good idea if I went and talked to one of the base chaplains. I said, "All I really need is the base gym and some time with God, and I will be fine." With that, I went into a mental cave in which the only things that existed in my world were God, studying, and pushing as much weight in that gym as was humanly possible.

Due to my new focus, I think one of the first miracles I ever experienced was at my training school. It may not seem like a miracle to most people, but for the first time in my life, I received awards for academic achievement. So at this point in my life, no one could ever tell me that prayer doesn't work. I received the award of honor grad with the highest GPA in my class. I had received many awards for athletic achievements, but this was a first for me.

**

In the last week of our training school, all the airmen who were graduating received orders to their next military assignment. Like everyone else, I had high hopes as to where I would be going. When my orders were released, I found I was going to be stationed in the Midwest, about an hour and a half from where my dad and stepmother and stepbrothers lived and about an hour's drive to my half brother and his wife's house. In some aspects, I thought this could be a good thing, but obviously, in other ways, it stirred up thoughts from my past that

I really didn't want to unearth. On one hand, I was happy that I was going to be so close to my half brother, but in truth I really didn't know what to expect from my dad and stepmom.

My First Assignment

Coming from a very large city, I was now being stationed in a town so small that it didn't even have a traffic light; just one four-way stop. It seemed to be miles and miles of nothing but trees and hills. The closest town to us was a small college town about twenty minutes away, population about sixteen thousand. Compared to the town where our base was, where the population at that time was under two thousand, this was going to take some getting used to. The work out and weight-training facilities on this new base was not as good as the one on my training base. I would make the best of it, and I still had my plate weights, which I had brought from the previous base to use in my room when needed.

Looking back on my time at this base, I really did enjoy it. I was able to reconnect with my half brother and get to know him and his family. Also, I got to know my half brother's cousin, an incredible person who had many different talents, one of which was that he had his own martial arts school, and he was a schoolteacher, musician, and magician on the side. It was the martial arts that I became very interested in. My half brother and his cousins had trained for quite some time together and were incredibly talented, so most of the time that I was in the Midwest at this particular military base, I would study martial arts under the guidance of my cousin. It went hand in hand with my weightlifting, and according to my cousin, I learned very fast.

As for my dad and stepmom, I had anticipated that it was going to be awkward. The demonic spirits that I had no name for when I was a kid were still with them. They seemed to be burdening them with the same problems they had always dealt with; only now it was about ten years later. My stepmom seemed to be doing much worse. I have no doubt that carrying around the demonic entities that she had become so used to was taking its toll on her health, as well as her mental state. By this time she was on many different medications. Most everyone was under the impression that she was a severe hypochondriac. Even doctors would prescribe her placebos, just to make her happy. Anytime a doctor would say that he was finding nothing wrong with her, she would get very angry and state that the doctor had no idea what he was talking about. She had also started smoking heavily. I am sure that this was contributing to her health problems, but most of us just stayed quiet to try to stay on her good side.

Sometimes she would seem to get some enjoyment out of throwing in my face the fact that my ex-wife had annulled our marriage and that I would probably never get married again. She proclaimed that if I did, it would only end in divorce anyway. My dad would argue with her about her health problems, but that just made it harder for him to live there with her, so after some time, he just gave up trying to say anything about it.

My half brother, when he would visit, would talk to her as well about her health problems. It seemed to me that everyone who came in contact with her was forced to walk on eggshells, and at no time was the elephant in the room ever addressed.

When I was allowed to, I would try to talk to them about God. I would say that they really didn't need to carry around the same backpacks full of problems for the rest of their lives. I have no doubt they could have laid those issues down at the foot of the cross and been burden free. But sometimes I think that the devil makes us believe that we are to carry these burdens around forever, that we can never be forgiven. If you have ever read the word, Satan is the father of lies. He has come to steal, kill, and destroy, and only if we give him permission can he obtain his goal.

My dad asked me to forgive him for how things turned out when I was younger. He said that even when my stepmom had accused me of things, in his heart he knew they had never happened, and he was right. But what it did was give him and my stepmom an excuse to leave Southern California, which was where my mom and family were, and return to the Midwest, where my stepmom wanted to go back to, to be closer to her kids and family.

It was never really talked about, but I always felt that my stepmom would take out her aggression toward my mom on me, even as a young man. I had very little doubt that if she could have ended my life and gotten away with it, she would have. She would act so nice when my half brother or stepbrothers were in the house, or when her grandkids would come to visit, but whenever it was just her and me, she was a whole different person; even her language would change to profanity. Sometimes my dad would hear her say things and almost not even recognize her voice, as if demonic entities were given permission to use her as a host to come after me. It seemed like a bipolar disorder, except that it was only I who would bring out this awful side of her.

I have no doubt that my three sisters would probably agree with me on this, and I think their solution to the problem was probably much better than mine, which was to keep their distance from my stepmother. They would call my dad on the phone, which allowed them to stay in touch and not have to interact with his wife.

I really did want to make an attempt to reconnect with my dad. After all, when I was young, he was not just my dad; he was my coach and probably my best friend. However, the price I had to pay each time I came to visit their house was far too high, and when I would return back to my base, I would seem to struggle with the same things that I had struggled with when I was a child under her authority. As much as I enjoyed spending time getting to know this side of my family, I knew I needed to get far away from this place.

Most of my friends on the military base were coworkers, people I knew from the fitness center, or people at the dormitory where I lived. I had no close friends, but as always, I seemed to be friends with most everyone. Sometimes when I was by myself, I would think about what I would be doing if my now ex-wife were here. Would we be decorating our house? Or maybe going off for a car ride through the trees and hills? Maybe finding lakes or ponds and doing some fishing, or visiting my half brother and his wife? I would then come back to reality and realize that there were really not many people who actually cared a whole lot about me. I really wanted to reconnect with a church, but there was no real church off base, so once again, I had to rely on the base chapel. I still to this day do not know how to sing out of a hymnal, and other than "Amazing Grace," I didn't actually get much out of the services. But I went anyway. I had plenty of time to read my Bible and to lift weights.

Sometimes, God would allow me to see things so that I could connect and maybe even witness to the people around me. I had a conversation with my roommate once when I was allowed to see into the spirit. He had been struggling with things in his hometown, with his family. I was shown some specific things to tell him—things that I had no way of knowing. When I told him that God had showed me these things, he dismissed it and felt that I had overheard him talking on the phone in the dorm or that somehow he had talked about it in his sleep. He couldn't accept the fact that God cared enough about him to make me aware and to try to help them through the situation. Some people would say things like "Am I making it that obvious, by the way I'm acting?" or "Boy, you're really good at reading people's thoughts."

I would say, "Actually, God just cares enough about you to tell someone who can maybe help."

But most of the time, I felt like a firefighter trying to put out a blaze with a bucket of water. For every one person God allowed me to help, it seemed as if there were ten who didn't want to hear anything I had to say, and often the response was

"You know this is really none of your business, so keep your thoughts to yourself, and leave me alone." I would try to tell them these were not my thoughts at all. God just cares enough about you to give some insight to me.

***

I was frustrated with my situation, but mostly due to my stepmother. It felt as if the first time she came into my life, she did whatever she could to get as far away from me as possible.

But this time, it was I who wanted to put some distance between us, so I decided to put in for orders to another base. It would take some time for me to actually leave, so I took a gamble and put in for worldwide remote, which means you can go anywhere the military decides to send you. I'm sure that my dad and half brother didn't really understand this, and I was pretty used to keeping things to myself. Trusting people with the truth or my thoughts had very rarely ever panned out for me, especially when it came to my family. By this time, months had passed, and I had tried again and again to reconnect the relationship with my dad. There were times where we were together, sometimes driving around, or even fishing with my dad, my half brother, and me. These were times when it felt as if I had my dad back, but they were all too often short lived, and my stepmom would come back into the picture. At those times, I couldn't get away fast enough.

Before I knew it, I had my next assignment. I would be going to a military base in Germany, and for me, I couldn't leave fast enough.

Chapter 7

Going to a foreign country was very enlightening as well as fascinating. From the moment I came into the country, I wanted to learn as much as I possibly could. After all, my last name was of German descent. Just the history of the European continent was so incredible to me, even though there was a wall separating East and West Berlin. Even that was a fascinating part of history.

After going to my duty section and being introduced to my coworkers, I was placed in a dorm several miles away from the military base where I was assigned. Obtaining a European driver's license was going to be critical. There was a bus system, but whenever possible, you would try to ride with a friend. The people in Germany were very friendly to the military members. It was as if we left our own country, where the military was discriminated against, and came to a foreign country, where they seemed to appreciate what the American servicemen had done for their country. We were even told that if an older German citizen stood in the gutter when we walked up on the sidewalk, to just not say anything, because what they were actually doing was showing us respect for liberating their country during World War II. They would even give us preferential treatment when we went to eat at different restaurants.

I told myself that this was a new beginning, and I was going to try to do things differently from what I had done at my last base.

I knew that God had given me this gift to help people, but I felt as if I was helping pretty much no one. So taking a page out of my past, I was going to do my best to stay silent on my ability to see into the spirit. I did try going to the base chapel. There were several to choose from, but all of them were about the same as those I had known at my other bases—as if they were just going through the motions of church, not wanting to offend anyone. I sensed in the spirit that the service was flat. I didn't yet speak the language, so it wasn't as if I could go downtown and go to church, although it seemed as if the German people would've welcomed me. So I just kept to myself and read my Bible. For now, that would have to be good enough.

The problem was, the spiritual gift that I had been given wasn't easily turned off. It wasn't like someone who had the gift of singing and just chose not to sing. I could still see as God allowed me to, and sometimes as much as I wanted to turn it off, I never seemed to have control of that switch.

I was also blessed with a very good roommate, and even though he outranked me, he said I intimidated him due to my size. By this time I was up to about 215 pounds, and when I wasn't working, I was lifting weights. On the military base, we were allowed to play many sports, such as American football, baseball, basketball, and wrestling. I am sure there were other sports available, but these were the only ones that I paid attention to. These were military base functions, and for our base, it included army as well as air force. Somehow, they already knew that I could play some outside linebacker, and they were quick to recruit me onto the American football team.

***

This was not flag football. This was full pads, as well as full-contact football at about the same level as the college football that I had played in California. In truth, the talent level was actually much better than where I played college football. The reason why I use the term American football is because in Europe they call soccer football as well, so when we were overseas, we would have to make a distinction between the two.

This was an activity that I was already used to, and because I was on the base team, they would allow me extra time in the gym, as well as muscle-building supplements that weren't available to everyone. They were also able to work out a deal with my squadron to move my weight limit up to

225 pounds, which for me was great, because it allowed me to gain about 10 more pounds of muscle weight. However, one of my coaches said that they might have to move me to a different squadron to maintain this weight waiver.

My roommate informed me that the football team seemed to be something like a rock star on base; we were on a very large military base, and everyone stationed there came out to football games to support their teams. So if your name was called very often during the game, when you are off field, everyone knew who you were. He and some of the other residents in the dorm we lived in had already named me BMOC. I had heard terms like this before, but I didn't really know what this one meant. I was informed that it was "Big Man on Campus." According to him, he liked going placcs with me because he said people treated him differently when I was with him. He said that I didn't notice it because I was so used to it. To me, everybody treated me well, and I seemed to get along with everyone.

Of course, this also meant that they wanted me to go to the airmen's club with them because, as they put it, "we travel with our own personal bouncer." But what I already knew was that once guys started getting a few too many beers, they would get brave, demonic entities would start whispering in their ears, and the next thing you would know, there was trouble. It wasn't really like me to fight. I would just break it up, hoping no one would get in trouble or get hurt.

After being in country for a few months, I obtained a European driver's license, and my own car.

***

In my free time, another thing I liked to do, other than lift weights, was to drive around this fascinating country and find old buildings. If I was lucky, there were demonic entities who thought they could intimidate me. Most of the time, I would revert back to when I was younger and see if they would talk to me. Most of these entities had never come across a seer, but I felt that all of them knew that in Jesus's name I could at any time cast them out. Acts 19:15 talks about an evil spirit that said, "Jesus I know, Paul I know, but who are you?" These evil spirits sensed that I knew my authority, but at this point in time, I didn't really understand that if I were to cast them out, they would come back and inhabit this building at a later time. So I would try to engage them in conversation, and most of the time they would say something like "Do what you have come to do and leave us alone."

Being naïve, I would ask them questions like "How long have you been here?" Or "Why are you here?" Sometimes they would try to play games with me or ask if they could come with me. I would try to sound all spiritual and say something like "Where I am going you cannot come."

In response to that, they would reply, "Why not?"

At this point in time, I really wasn't that good at this sort of stuff, and when I got tired of it, I would just say, "In Jesus's name, I cast you out," and that was pretty much it.

Of course, when I went back to the dorm, people would ask me, "So, what have you been doing?"

I would say, "Just driving around looking at the countryside. You should try it. There are some pretty cool buildings out there."

They didn't really think anything of it, and I never let them think anything different. In fact, most of them just thought I liked being by myself, and this had worked for me in the past.

Touring History in Europe

At least once a month, some of my friends and I would make it a point to go visit a different country. Of all the things I did while living in Germany, this was probably the best idea. I had learned to speak some of the language, and in most of the countries we visited, we would all try to learn a few words so that we wouldn't be helpless. I had always loved learning about history, but now I was actually walking in places that I had only read about. I always liked to go on in-depth tours when I would first visit a new country. That way, I could map out things that I wanted to do and see when I came back on my own.

Knowing that it was possible to interact with entities that had been in these buildings, homes, and castles for who knows how many years was fascinating to me. I was well known for getting lost during tours because I wanted to see what was there in the spirit as well as what was there in the natural. I was very rarely disappointed because for whatever reason, demonic entities attach themselves to buildings and places. When I was younger, I had spent the night in what was said to be a haunted house, but that was small potatoes in comparison to spending the night in a so-called haunted castle. There was always some part of me that thought that just maybe one of these places I went to was actually haunted by something like a ghost, but it was always just a demonic entity that was manifesting itself into something that it thought would invoke fear. I have to admit, from time to time, they would catch me off guard and startled me, but once I realized what it was I was dealing with, then it was just my own curiosity.

***

One of my coworkers and his wife enjoyed
traveling around Europe. Most of the airmen I knew
just wanted to stay in the dorms on the weekends
and maybe chase girls at the airman's club. But I
was more interested in traveling to new places that I
had only heard about in history books. So, much of
the time I would travel with my friend and his wife.
She always wanted to go to Paris, and traveling by
way of the Autobahn, we were only an hour or so
drive away. On this trip, we would see different
sites in Paris, France, the first of which was the
palace of Versailles, King Louis XIV's royal
residence. We also visited common sites such as the
Eiffel Tower. When we went to the Louvre
Museum, it turned out to be a pretty incredible
place. The paintings, artwork, and sculptures were
absolutely incredible. What I wasn't expecting was
the demonic entities, which I'm pretty sure our tour
guide knew very little about. What I found out from
our guide was that the Louvre in 1190 was a battle
fortress, and in the sixteenth century, it was a royal
palace of King Louis XIV. I'm not really sure if
what I was seeing in the spirit had to do with the
battle fortress or the royal palace, but I was certain
that there were demonic entities attached to this
historical museum.

It was a little hard for me to wander off, between the tour guide and security in the museum, but in some of the rooms that were roped off to the public, I could see some very familiar entities moving about.

When Paris really became interesting for me was when we went to Notre Dame Cathedral, built between the twelfth and fourteenth centuries. This was seemingly a wellspring of spiritual activity. Because this was a church, you would have expected for me to see angelic activity. On the contrary, judging from the gargoyles that seemed to cover the entire structure, I sensed a much darker past. As we walked up through the cobblestone courtyard in front of the cathedral, my friend's wife pointed out dark spots in the brickwork that we were walking on. Something told me to put my hand there, and I could feel a cold darkness and sensed that many people had died in the shadows of this historic structure. Even though there were tourists walking about in the courtyard, there were demonic entities mixed in, moving about unnoticed. Some of them were moving up the sides of the building and into windows. It was hard for me to understand what they were doing, but without a doubt, very little seemed to be slowing them down.

I told my friends that I was curious to go inside the structure and look around. They agreed, and we all went in. At first, I thought it was interesting that they had put some of the gargoyles inside the cathedral as well, but as I looked closer, they were, in fact, demonic entities that were perched in a squatting position, looking down into the building. When they did move from their perched positions, they moved very slowly, as if they didn't want to be noticed. Some of the demonic entities had even taken on the forms of the gargoyles from the outsides of the building. One seemed to look right at me and follow me across the room. Once my friends and I reached the main part of the cathedral, I felt as if there were at least a hundred eyes following me. It could have been my own paranoia, or the possibility that this building had a much different past than most would think.

After touring through the inner workings of Notre Dame, we went back outside. I stopped and began taking a better look at the gargoyles that were perched throughout this incredible structure and realized that many of these gargoyles posted on the outside of the building were in fact demonic entities that had manifested themselves to look like gargoyle statues. For whatever reason, taking position from this vantage point allowed them to have an unobstructed view of the city of Paris— north, south, east, and west, as well as overseeing the Seine River, which runs next to Notre Dame. With this viewpoint, I think they somehow felt that they had dominion over this city in France and were feeling secure because they had been there for thousands of years, never being tested nor cast out. Their presence was secure as long as they stayed inhabitants of this famous structure.

***

Traveling throughout Europe was a way to see parts of the world and was also a great way to spend my time. A group of friends I worked with decided to go visit London, England. The countryside was beautiful, but to a degree a dreary place. We weren't able to walk around as I would usually do; instead we took a tour on a double-decker bus, which was nice because we were able to see most of the sites in a short amount of time.

The only demonic entities I encountered were the ones I saw on the sides of the road, on occasion walking with people. At one point, I saw a small group and unfortunately, I said something like "Wow, look at that." Then I thought, "Did I say that out loud?" I'm sure the people around me just assumed I had seen something that they had not. Even being a passenger on this bus was strange to me. Driving on the wrong side of the road could have been detrimental to my health, so it was a good thing we did not try to drive there.

***

On the way back to our military base in Germany, we decided to take a detour and see the Berlin Wall. When we arrived, we parked our car and walked along the wall. Now, as you walked along in West Berlin, the wall itself was a mass of graffiti, and there were sidewalks so that you could walk right next to it. There were even viewing areas so that you could peer into East Berlin. On the eastern side, the wall was clean and untouched by any spray paint, and there was a large dirt field—as a guess, I would say about a hundred yards across. It looked as if there wasn't even a weed growing. And on the other side of that, a large chain-link fence and guards. That was when I saw something in the clearing. At first, I thought it was an animal running across the blank field of dirt, so I started watching it. I even made the mistake of asking one of my friends what he thought it was.

He said, "I don't see anything."

I thought that was strange. And again I saw what looked like an animal running in this blank field, and once again, I pointed and said, "That."

With his blank stare, I realized that I might be the only one seeing it, so I did my best to just play it off as if it were nothing. For the next twenty minutes, I watched these demonic entities run back and forth across this empty field, never really understanding what they were doing and why. It wasn't as if I had anybody who could explain it to me, so for now, it was just going to be a mystery to me.

***

On yet another weekend, we decided to go visit the small country of Luxenberg, with large rolling hills and green as far as the eye could see. Luxenberg was known as having the most bridges in the world per capita. For an American military man, one of the most sobering sites to see is the World War II American war cemetery, where General George S. Patton is buried along with 5,076 American service members, most from Patton's US Third Army. The memorial cemetery often had many visitors, but on more than fifty acres of land, you could get lost in thought reading the many crosses that cover these green hills in Luxenberg.

As I walked, I lost track of some of the people I had come with, so I looked around. I noticed there were several figures walking through the cemetery as well. They stood out to me because even though it was daytime, there was an unusual light shining all the way around them. Sometimes they would come together, as if to speak to one another, but more often than not, they were walking about the cemetery on their own. Being curious and a little nosy, I kept reading the cross-shaped headstones while moving toward the shining entities. As I got closer, I thought they would start moving away from me, but they didn't. I approached one of them and stood right next to one. Doing what I could to strike up a conversation, I said, "So, what do you think?"

The individual looked up at me and said, "You are a seer. What do you think?"

I said, "I would like to think that most of these men who gave their lives for our country are in a much better place, a place of peace and joy that is void of pain and sorrow."

The glowing entity said to me, "Seer, you have spoken wisely. Most of these men knew the Lord and are at this moment dressed in robes of salvation."

I asked, "So why are you here?"

The angel of the Lord said, "We are here to comfort the souls of the mourners who have come to pay tribute to their fallen brothers and sisters in answer to the prayers that have been prayed by their loved ones."

As tears ran down my face, one of the couples I had traveled with came to me and handed me a Kleenex. The wife said, "This place has a way of getting to you."

I said, "You have no idea."

This trip would stay etched in my mind for quite some time, because in my life, the demonic entities that I had come in contact with far outnumbered the angels that I had encountered. But I would trust God that he had been preparing me for things that would take place in my future. In this I had absolute faith.

***

Many of the tours to see Europe were packages that were offered from the recreation center on base from what was called ITT tours. On one such trip, I took a week of leave from the military and booked a trip to Italy. This was one of those places that I had always dreamed of visiting. It was often talked about in the Bible, and to see some of these places was, for me, a once-in-a-lifetime experience.

in Rome, as you might guess, the first place we visited was the Coliseum. The great thing about this particular tour was that they would take us to the sites, and if we wanted to tour with them, we could, but they would let us wander short distances from the group. The moment we walked into the Coliseum, it was a mixture of emotion to know that Christians like me had been put to the ultimate act of faith and their demise in this legendary arena. The wood deck flooring that was covered with dirt had long ago rotted away, exposing the holding cells for the Christians, gladiators, and unwilling participants of this brutal day and age.

In this place, well known by most people in the world, God allowed me to see things that for most people would never come into view. I have no doubt that thousands of years ago, angels inhabited the prison cells to bring peace and comfort to those who were about to die for their faith, but in this day and age, all I could see in the spirit was a sparse number of demonic entities moving about where spectators had once sat. On occasion, they would move about among the ruins that had once been holding cells. I couldn't help but think how many of my brothers and sisters in heaven today came there by way of this arena for the entertainment of the masses who looked on with no remorse, no empathy, and no regard for the pain that was caused to create this medium of entertainment. As we walked around where the spectators had once sat, I couldn't help but imagine the sights that had been seen here, and angrily, under my breath, I cast out demons as they appeared to me. I had no doubt that they would probably return at some point once my presence was no longer there, but I felt confident that other Christians would sense their presence and once again cast them out.

After leaving the Coliseum, we went to Circus Maximus, which was similar to the site I had just left but with far fewer demonic entities. We were allowed to walk onto the ground floor of this arena, which had been the inspiration of many movies. Demonic entities of fear would attempt to re-create the same sense of panic that must've been felt by the victims here; the other tourists were laughing and re-creating the horse-drawn chariots that for years raced around this historic place. I could still sense the darkness and the pain that must've overtaken some of these unwilling participants.

Then we went to tour Caesar's Palace, which for the most part was just ruins, possibly destroyed by modern bombs. There was very little left.

Luckily, after that, we went back to our rooms to relax, swim in the pool, and eat. My mind was still trying to comprehend once again how human beings could cause so much pain to their fellow man with no remorse. This was very hard for me to understand.

***

The next day we were to go to the Vatican, the Sistine Chapel, and St. Peter's Cathedral. I thought this would be a welcome change from the demonic sites I'd seen the previous day.

On coming into the Vatican, we were shown the traditional Swiss Guard. I felt pretty confident that I wouldn't have to look at nearly as many demonic entities, and I even hoped to get a glimpse of the incredible architecture and the famous works of Michelangelo, as well as a once-in-a-lifetime opportunity to see in the spirit one or two angelic entities in this amazing place.

One of the first places that stands out in my mind is the Sistine Chapel. There were not many people walking around because it was on a weekday, so it was not as crowded as it could've been on a weekend. But as I walked and did my best to capture in photographs this indescribable site, I once again noticed that many of the people, most of whom were not with groups and were without cameras, were standing by themselves near the walls, with a familiar glow surrounding them. Not really knowing everyone in my group, I made a comment and asked one of my friends if the guy over there standing next to the wall was with us in our group. My friend said, "I don't know. Why?"

I said, "Well, he doesn't have a camera, and I thought I would ask him if he wanted me to get a picture of him in the Sistine Chapel."

My friend said, "How would I know? Go ask him."

For whatever reason, I smiled and thought, "Maybe I'm not the only one who can see in the spirit. It very well could be that I'm the only one who knows what I'm looking at."

So after getting the pictures I wanted, including included pictures of the Sistine Chapel, and knowing good and well that some of these people I had seen glowing were the focal point of the pictures, all I wanted to know was, Will they show up in my photographs?

With that, I walked over to a place by the wall next to what I felt sure was an angelic being and tried to engage in a conversation. I said, "From across the room, these tapestries on the sidewalls look like real drapes. It's hard to see it when you're standing next to it. Have you walked out into the middle of the room and looked back at these?"

The gentleman looked at me and with a smile said, "You are a seer, and I'm sure you know the answer to your own question." Then he started to walk, and turning around, he said, "Walk with me, seer."

I smiled and thought, "Just yesterday I could feel the pain of thousands and thousands of Christians. How is it possible that today I am blessed to walk among angels? Only by God's hand can this be."

Once we reached the front wall of the Sistine Chapel, this angelic being began to explain to me some of the intricacies of what Michelangelo was depicting on this incredible canvas. His words will stay with me always. And right on cue, as he finished speaking, our tour guide called us back together. As we walked out of this incredible place, the gentleman leading our group informed us that next we would be going to St. Peter's Basilica.

***

In the Vatican, just walking through the hallways going from point A to point B was breathtaking. Sometimes it was hard to take in everything I was seeing. Books could do this incredible place very little justice, and in my mind, unless you are able to witness it in person, it would be hard to explain or understand. Coming to St. Peter's Basilica, the first word that came to mind was *massive*. It was much larger than I had anticipated, but the details of even the smallest items were incredible. Looking down into St. Peter's final resting place took my breath away. I could feel the presence of God, but I was unable to discern any angelic presence in the basilica. I was hoping to have another experience like the one in the Sistine Chapel. I have no doubt that the presence was there, and it was probably I who failed to recognize it.

***

In the following days we traveled to Naples, Italy, which was beautiful, and the food was amazing as well. And then on to the island of Capri, which seemed magical with the blue waters and the amazing people. I had no doubt that someday I would return to see this place again.

Then we traveled to Pompeii, which, if you don't know, was buried by a volcano (Mount Vesuvius) under a thick carpet of volcanic ash while the city was inhabited in 79 AD. Pompeii was a much larger city than I had thought, and for the time, it was very modern for a Roman city. All its inhabitants who were in the city were buried in the ash, dying instantly, both man and beast. Maybe it was because of the volcano still looming in the distance or just the thought of what had taken place there, but a sense of fear still seemed to be present. And even though it was broad daylight, it still felt dark. In the shadows of some of the buildings I could once again see demonic entities moving about. As my curiosity would draw me in their direction, they appeared to keep their distance. I would quietly and under my breath tell them to leave this place in Jesus's name, and as always, they would go; but something in my soul told me that my authority was partially limited to my being there in that place.

I sat down in what I was told was a marketplace. I had brought a pocket Bible with me (Psalms, Proverbs, and the New Testament) and began to read. As I did, I felt peace in my heart that I was not the first person to sit in this marketplace and read the word of God, and I hoped I would not be the last.

***

On the last day of our trip, we traveled to Pisa, where the Leaning Tower is, as well as Florence. In Pisa, there is a cathedral on the same site, as well as a baptistry and a bell tower, which, if you don't know, is what the Leaning Tower of Pisa is. Spiritually speaking, I didn't sense much there, but we were only able to go into the Leaning Tower and not the cathedral and the baptistry.

Other than the entities that I noticed with other tourists, I saw very little except the beautiful structures that existed in the natural. In Florence, there were extremely large churches that were sterile in the spirit inside, but there were small churches throughout the city that seemed to be overflowing with angelic activity. One such church was Basilica di Santa Croce, which is the burial place of Michelangelo, Galileo, Machiavelli, and hundreds of others, as it was in the Sistine Chapel. It was also here that angelic beings were moving about in the crowd. In this smaller church with so many people, I felt that approaching any of them was not a good idea, so I just observed them from afar, some interacting with tourists, who had no idea whom they were entertaining. I have no question that the words and the insight that was given were profound. Even people who were in our group entertained some of these entities, and I was curious to ask them what the conversation was.

Do You See What I See?

The couple I had traveled with on several occasions, a coworker of mine, asked me if I would like to go on a trip with him and his wife. They were going to one of the concentration camps in Germany, Dachau. I had mixed feelings about visiting one of these camps. In truth, I really didn't know what to expect. But I agreed to go on the trip with them. And as we parked the car and walked into the camp, for a person who had grown up seeing demonic spirits, this was an eerie place. At one point I had to stop, to just try to comprehend the horrific things that had taken place here. Not just the death. It was more than that. It was more about how a human being could be so void of empathy for a fellow human being as to commit these heinous acts of violence—the so-called scientific testing; taking machine guns and just level entire groups of human beings. I had seen many things that most will never even know exist, but the weight of this place was so incredibly heavy on my spirit.

My friend and his wife asked me if I was going to be OK. I told them to go ahead and go on in, and as soon as I could get past this moment, I would be right behind them. In some ways, I was so overwhelmed it seemed as if there were thousands of demonic spirits. My eyes were closed, and I had just barely walked into the camp. What would it possibly be like going into these buildings? Was I even ready for this, spiritually speaking? I had not had much fellowship, and about all I was able to do was read my Bible and pray.

I continued to walk in, and as I made it past the doorway, the weight seemed to get heavier. Breathing was rather difficult. It was hard to make out what I was seeing at first. It was just darkness, figures moving about the room. In truth, I was unable to even see them as figures. All it looked like was types of shadows moving about. It was almost as if there was just too much going on for me to quite comprehend. Looking back, I should have just started casting things out.

***

It was in that first building that a girl walked up to me and asked, "Are you OK?"

Trying to act as if everything was OK was easier said than done, but I was trying to be cool about it.

She watched me for a minute, and then she said something that caught me off guard. She said, "Can you see?"

In truth, I didn't know what to say to her, so I just returned the question. "Can you see?"

She kind of smiled and said, "That depends on what you're seeing." Then she walked to the middle the room and said, "Walk over here and tell me what you see."

So I walked over.

As she pointed, I said, "There's a group of entities crouched in the corner of that room, and for whatever reason, there's a pile of demonic entities in this room as well. Why? What do you see?"

She just smiled and said, "You're some type of seer, aren't you?"

I was reluctant to answer that question, so I looked in a different room and pointed and said, "What do you see?"

She said, "It's really the same thing in most of the rooms. The little demons just crouched and moving about seem to be afraid of you. Are you one of those Christians?"

I said, "I am a Christian. Why?"

She said, "Are you a Christian with dominion over demonic spirits, or are you a Christian because you think that's what I want to hear?"

I was kind of new at this, and I still wasn't sure if she could see in the spirit. It was possible that she knew there were demonic entities there. After all, it had been a German concentration camp, and as a seer, what else would you expect to see?

The couple had come with came back to the room where I was.

My coworker said, "So you found a friend."

She smiled and said, "Why yes, he has."

He and his wife said they would go on ahead, but with a smile said they would keep an eye on us.

I asked, "So we're friends?"

She said, "More like kindred spirits." Then she asked me how long I had been seeing in the spirit.

I said, "Since I was a kid."

She said that she had been seeing in the spirit since she was young as well; then she asked me if I thought they were scary.

She said, "When I was a child, they would scare me."

I asked, "What would they do to scare you?"

She said, "They would get real close to my face and try to talk to me, and their breath smelled like sulfur. Most of the time I didn't want to talk, but it didn't matter which way I turned my face. They were still there. So finally, I would just put my hands over my face and sit on the floor until they went away." She asked, "Did they ever do that to you?"

I said, "Yes, but I found something out by accident when I was young."

She asked, "What was that?"

I answered, "Psalm 23. Every time I would start speaking this verse, they would move away from me, like I was in a bubble."

She said, "That's true. They don't really like it when you start speaking from the Bible."

We started walking through the different buildings in the concentration camp. There were pictures of these prisoners of war. There were also pictures of piles of dead bodies. Among everything else that was going through my mind, I had to wonder about the person who had taken these pictures. Why would you want to permanently document these terrible acts?

My new friend asked me if these same demonic entities had ever allowed me to do different things, such as move objects across the room or levitate. I said yes, when I was younger, but only because I didn't know any better.

She said, "That's right. You're a Christian, so all you can do with the demons now is cast them out."

I asked her, "So let me guess. You're still entertaining these demonic entities, the same entities that caused all of this to take place, everything around us, this entire camp and all of the buildings. This was done through demonic spirits who deceived an entire country. I don't really think you want to play with entities that tried to destroy an entire race of people."

She said, "Well, that was a long time ago, and besides that, if you cast them out, they won't let you do fun things."

I asked her, "So I'm guessing you are not a Christian."

She said, "Well, my parents are, and they said that God has given me a gift. I have to admit they have always supported me and allowed me to speak my mind on what I was seeing, but it seems to me that it's a lot more fun to let them stay around and do things. How is casting them out any fun at all?"

I asked her, "Have you ever cast one out?"

She said, "No, and I really don't want to. I'm not even sure I can. It's not like I can call myself a Christian or anything."

She went on to tell me that she had been raised in church but had never really accepted it. It was more of a Sunday-morning ritual that she and her family always did. Her pastor knew she could see in the spirit, but she said that she didn't like talking about it to him. Sometimes she would open up to her mom, and she was told that she had a very special gift from God. She said to her mom when she was a teenager, "Why would God give me something I didn't want?"

Her mom's response was "You will need to pray to God and ask him to reveal to you why you have this gift."

I'm guessing she never did.

***

She was now a staff sergeant in the US Air Force, also stationed at a base in Germany. She had been there for quite some time and spoke the language fairly well. She was a couple of years older than I was and also outranked me. I was only an A1C, more commonly known as an airman. She wasn't really that interested in me, other than the fact we were both seers. At one point, while we were in the concentration camp, she took hold of my hand. I said, "You're not afraid, are you?"

She smiled and said, "No, but there are your friends, and I thought it would give you guys something to talk about on the way home."

I thought, "What am I getting myself into?" But still I was intrigued.

My new friend and I hadn't walked around the camp that much, and when my coworker and his wife walked up to us, they asked what all we had seen in the camp.

I said, "Not a whole lot."

We were still in the main building, so we walked along behind them as they showed us different things. They were looking at it as if they were reading the pages of a history book, once in a while commenting that "this is so sad." My new friend and I stayed back far enough so that we could still talk to each other without being heard by others, and by the sound of it, she had been there several times before and knew the grounds well. I couldn't tell if she enjoyed being around this incredibly large group of demonic entities or what.

***

At one point, we stopped where there was a bunch of bathrooms that the Germans had used as a makeshift gas chamber. She said, "Watch this!" As I looked in, I saw a group of demonic entities heaped in a pile with a few stragglers here and there. She said, "I cast you out!"

The demonic entities looked at her and then looked at one another, and one of them started to walk up to her. Then it stopped about halfway and looked at me.

The demon said, "Seer."

My friend said, "Cool. They know your name. They don't say that to me."

Then she said, "You cast them out."

I said, "Why? I thought you like them here."

She said, "They don't really bother me, so I don't really see a point. But I have been told that as a Christian, you supposedly have dominion over them. So do you?"

I said, "I have nothing over them but by way of the name that is above all names. I have been given power and authority through Jesus Christ. That's what I have. So if you ask me if I can cast them out, I on my own, can do nothing."

Then I looked at the demonic entities and said, "In the name of Jesus Christ of Nazareth, I cast you out. You must leave."

At that, they just moved away, and the room was clear except for what was physically left there, which was still a tragedy.

She said, "You are the first person I've ever seen do that. My parents told me that I could, but I never really wanted to."

I said, "If you want me to, I can walk you through the salvation prayer, found in Romans 10:9, and then you can cast them out as well".

She said, "Maybe someday, but not today."

***

This particular friend and I would spend quite a bit of time together while on our tour in Germany. We were both there by way of the military, and even though most people called her my girlfriend, the truth was she liked big, burly biker-type guys with longer hair and beards. I wasn't exactly her type, but she did like the fact that we both were able to see in the spirit. So with that common thread, there were certain things she liked doing with me. I was OK with that. We had mutual friends, even though we worked in completely different functions on base. She was in administrations under one of the squadron commanders, and by this time I had been cross-trained out of the Maintenance Squadron into the SOS Squadron. So, in short, she was a paper pusher, and I was learning how to jump out of planes. This always confused my stepdad, who was a load master on a C 131. He would constantly ask me, "If the plane isn't going down, why are you jumping out?"

My only answer was "Because they told me to."

He would reply, "I think you may be listening to the wrong people. If the pilots weren't bailing out, then you shouldn't either."

I guess there was no arguing with that, but in the military, you do as you're told. I needed to keep my personal opinions to myself.

***

On one weekend, my so-called girlfriend and I were going with a group of our friends to see a movie in German. I didn't understand a lot of German words, but I could hold my own in a conversation. My girlfriend spoke very good German. Either way, it was always fun to go see movies where they were going to have to do voice-overs in German. We knew what most of the actors actually sounded like, so hearing them speaking in a foreign language was entertaining. The group wanted to go see one of the *Friday the 13th* movies. I looked at my girlfriend and said, "I don't think so."

She laughed and looked at the rest of the group and said, "He doesn't like that stuff."

One of the other guys in the group, trying his best to look cool in front of his girlfriend, said, "Why? Are you afraid?"

I said, "No, I just like action movies and comedies better."

Still trying to look cool in front of his girlfriend, he said, "I think the big weight lifter is scared!"

He was starting to irritate me, and being almost twice his size, I looked back at him and said, "You have no idea what scared looks like."

My girlfriend stepped into the conversation and said, "I have a great idea. How about tomorrow we take you somewhere and show you what scared looks like?"

The guy, still doing his best to show he was a man, said, "What do you have in mind?"

My girlfriend just said, "You'll see."

And with that, we went different directions. They went to see the German version of *Friday the 13th*, and my girlfriend and I went to see *Beverly Hills Cop* in German—much funnier than the original seen in the United States.

The next day, the same group of people, who were all curious as to where my girlfriend was taking them, said, "We are going to Berchtesgaden in the German Bavarian Alps." It was a little bit of a drive from where we were, but the group seemed to be excited. None of them, including me, had ever been there.

My girlfriend and I drove together in her car, which was enough to invoke fear in just about anyone, because she had a little two-door Mercedes-Benz and was constantly trying to see how fast it would go. On the drive, my girlfriend and I discussed a few things. First of all, why were we going to Berchtesgaden?

She said, "Eagle's Nest is there, and at the base of the mountain are barracks that were used by the Luftwaffe as well as SS soldiers. I have used these buildings before to scare, as you would say, big, burly, biker guys."

So that answered one of my questions. Another question that I was curious about was what she could see in the spirit. She never talked about seeing anything angelic, only demonic spirits. She said, "I don't know why I've never seen an angel. There were times with my parents when I would say I did, but that was just to make them feel better." She saw demons almost every day, kind of like I did when I was kid.

I explained to her that until I gave my life to the Lord, I saw demons pretty much every day; then, after becoming a Christian, it was only sometimes, maybe once a week or so.

She said that this sounded a lot like a famous movie that we had seen, talking about the dark side and the light side. She said, "No, we don't play with swords, but the rest of the story sounds pretty familiar, with the ability to move objects and many times knowing what people are thinking by way of the spirit."

Without saying anything, I began to think. I had gone from a place of seeing in the spirit almost every day. Once I made the decision to follow God, it seemed there was some sort of spiritual filter put into place so that I was only able to see when God allowed me to. The thing that scared me was that I was once again starting to see almost every day. Was this because of my lack of time hearing the word in church, as I did at home, or the lack of fellowship with other Christians? I still read the word and prayed most of the time, but I had no doubt that my walk with God wasn't as strong as it had been back home, or even in basic military training school. I suppose it also had something to do with my fascination with my so-called girlfriend. I was spending a lot more time in places where demonic entities were known to be, such as the trip we were going on today.

***

After arriving at Eagle's Nest, we took a tour and just admired the view of the countryside, but I knew that our friend with the ego just had to speak up and say something like "Well, this has been scary!"

And of course, my girlfriend smiled and pointed down an abandoned elevator shaft and said, "Just wait till we go down there."

The guy said, "I don't think the tour guides will let us go down there."

My girlfriend said, "That's true. We will have to drive back down the hill."

So we jumped in our cars and took a road that led to the area under Eagle's Nest. We could see the opening where the elevator shaft would have ended, and lo and behold, a short distance away, there were old abandoned buildings. We got out of our cars, and as the sun was about fifteen minutes from going down, my girlfriend said this was the perfect time to go in.

With flashlights in hand, we entered the first building. It had been covered in multiple layers of graffiti. One of the girls said, "I really don't want to do this."

And of course, one of the guys said, "Don't worry; I'll protect you."

So with flashlights on, we all went inside. In this first building were several broken tables, chairs, and desks. The windows had been smashed out, and it looked as if there had been one too many parties held there. There was trash, broken bottles, and debris on the floor, as well as graffiti covering the walls.

Our friend, who seemed to talk too much, said, "So, is this supposed to scare me?"

And as usual, he was unable to see what my girlfriend and I had already known was there. I know that I should have said or done something, but instead I just crossed my arms and leaned up against the wall. My girlfriend began to speak in a low tone under her breath as the rest just commented on how creepy the place was.

I couldn't help it. I said, "It's about to get a whole lot creepier."

With that, one of the tables started to move, with the legs of the table screeching across the floor.

One of the guys said, "She must have this place rigged."

My girlfriend laughed as one of the desks, weighing about 150 pounds, rose up off the floor and pinned that same guy against the wall. Chairs began to bounce up and down on the floor, producing a loud tapping noise. A bottle lifted from the floor and smashed against one of the walls.

By the time all this had taken place, the room was clear, and cars were being started outside. The only ones left in the room were my girlfriend and me, plus the poor guy screaming at the top of his lungs trying to push the desk away.

My girlfriend began to laugh as I stood there and shook my head. The poor guy was able to get himself free and ran out the door. A car circled back and picked him up.

My girlfriend, laughing, looked at me and said, "Now, isn't that more fun than casting them out?"

I said, "You're going to have some explaining to do when we see those guys again."

She said with a smile, "It's all rigged, you know."

***

On the way home, we had yet another discussion. She was upset that we were able to go to only one of the buildings before everyone decided to run. I asked her about the demonic entity that from time to

227

time I would see with her. She didn't really want to talk about it.

I said, "If you want, in Jesus's name, I can cast it out, but you're going to have to agree with me on this."

She said, "I don't know what I want, so for now let's just leave it alone." Then she said, "I have a question for you."

I said, "Go ahead."

She said, "Why is it that I don't see anything with you?"

I smiled and said, "I'm pretty sure you told me that you've never seen an actual angel, so what do you think you're going to see with me?"

She said, "Don't be playing that holier-than-thou card with me. Every once in a while, I've seen demonic entities talking in your ear as well."

The fact was, I knew she was right. There were times when I would listen to things that I knew were not God, and for whatever stupid reason, I chose to listen anyway. I knew what she was saying was true. In my heart, I thought that maybe I needed to go back home to Southern California and my pastor friend, to get my head and my heart back where they were supposed to be, focused on God. I told my girlfriend that maybe we should go to one of the chaplain services on base.

She laughed and said, "Do you see angels in the chaplain's services on base?"

I said, "No, not really, but at least I'm hearing the word of God."

She said, "You go by yourself. I don't really think those services actually help anyone. In fact, you, being a seer, could probably do a much better job behind the pulpit. I'm sure they'll never allow that to happen, because for the most part, they seem to be neither hot nor cold. Just my own observation."

I knew she was right, but still it was better than nothing, and maybe I should give it another chance this next weekend, maybe.

***

I have to believe that I was more susceptible to different influences at this point in my walk with God; I was starting to see in the spirit more and more as I did when I was younger. In my workplace, I began to see demonic activity as well as angelic beings. It bothered me, and I really wanted to say something to some of these people, but I wasn't sure how they would receive this type of insight.

One of my supervisors was a tech sergeant. In the spirit, I knew that he was struggling with alcohol and also his marriage. I approached him in his office at one point and asked to talk. He said, "Sure. Close the door."

I thought we had a close enough relationship for me to share some things that I was seeing. I really didn't want to tell him how I knew these things. I told him about his drinking and what I had seen in the spirit about his wife. I knew that this was going to go one of two ways. Either we would talk about it, or he would get mad and tell me it was none of my business.

He sat in his chair and leaned back and said, "Boy, I don't know where you're getting your information from, but I don't like gossip. And who do you think you are, coming in my office and telling me stuff like that. Get out of my office, and don't bring that junk back in here again, or I will give you paperwork. Do you understand me?"

I said, "Yes, sir," and I walked out of his office.

One of the staff sergeants stopped me and asked, "What was he yelling at you about?"

I said, "Just some things that I had noticed. I guess it's none of my business."

The staff sergeant said to me, "Well, I think he's under a lot of stress at home, and he may not be dealing with it very well, so I don't think he's actually mad at you. I wouldn't take it personally."

I tried not to take it personally, because my desire was to help people. For example, in Germany, prostitution was legal, and many of the guys in the dorm enjoyed these services, one of my friends especially. I'm sure that when he was younger, he dealt with this obsession in a fairly innocent way, but it had escalated to the point where he would go visit these establishments two or three times a week. He thought this was completely normal, and in fact, what he was dealing with was a generational curse handed down to him from his father and maybe further back than that. I didn't have much knowledge at that time of generational curses or the demons that caused them. All I knew and had been taught at this point was to cast them out in Jesus's name. This friend and I had talked about this many times, and he would assure me that he had things under control. I asked him at one point if his father had struggled with this same problem. He laughed and said, "Where do you think I learned it from?"

I asked him if we could pray together before he contracted some sort of sexually transmitted disease.

He laughed and said, "It's a little too late for that. I'm already getting shots."

I asked him if he had any plans to get married, and he said, "As long as the milk is for sale, I don't need to buy a cow."

I guess it's hard to argue with stupid logic like that. So needless to say, I reverted back to when I was younger and just shut my mouth.

It didn't seem that I was helping anyone, and my girlfriend laughed and said, "Why do you even try? They don't listen to you."

She said, "I have an idea that will cheer you up. I know of a castle in Liechtenstein that is supposed to be haunted by ghosts. I have always wanted to go there and see for myself, and this seems like the perfect opportunity. I can think of no one better to go with than you, my seer buddy." She said that it was actually a hotel that was supposed to be haunted, and people came from all over the world to see if they could spend the entire night. Even if you didn't, the festivities and the food were supposed to be wonderful.

I said, "So you and I are going to spend the night in a haunted hotel castle?"

She said, "Don't get any big ideas, because we will both have our own rooms."

I asked, "Is anyone else going with us, or just you and me?"

She said, "I think we have frightened our friends enough for a while. It would probably be best if it was just you and me."

So, through the recreation center's ITT office, we booked a cruise of all of the castles on the Rhine River. The cruise ended at this haunted hotel castle, and buses would pick us up and bring us home the next day. The cruise on the Rhine River was awesome, and as luck would have it, some of my friends were booked on the same trip. But I guess there was a wimp package so you wouldn't have to stay the night in the haunted hotel castle.

So, after the cruise, we all toured this haunted castle. Afterward, we sat down at a large table, and in true medieval fashion, they served us dinner. The only silverware we had was a knife. I don't think in the medieval days they had little wet towels for your hands, but we did, so we ate food from the middle of the table, something like family style. After dinner, we made fun of our friends as they left the castle on their bus to go home.

***

We were assigned rooms next to each other. The only heat source in the rooms was an open fireplace and lots of blankets. You were welcome to walk around the castle after hours as long as you didn't disturb anyone, and I had no doubt that my girlfriend and I were going to take advantage of that. As we settled into our rooms, she came and knocked on my door and asked if I was ready to go spelunking. She said she had heard rumors of where we were to go first, and as always, I was following.

Now, in the spirit, we both had noticed obviously demonic entities that were known to create fear, but what we were really looking for

were demonic entities of deception. These seemed
to be the ones that would try to manifest into
different images. I also wanted to see if there were
any demonic entities actually attached to this castle.
I felt really bad because another couple who had
been sitting next to us on the cruise asked if they
could come with us. I smiled and looked at my
girlfriend, and she said, "Sure. This will be fun."

I just shook my head and thought, "This
may not be a good idea."

The four of us walked through the hallways
of the castle. The funny thing was, the demonic
entity that generally created fear was near this guy
and not his girlfriend; he stayed in the back and
seemed to be ready to run at any second.

We went into a room, and there were suits of
armor along one wall. The rooms were lit by
candles, but we had been given flashlights to take
with us. During the tour of the castle, I had noticed
that all of the suits of armor were quite short, and in
this room, they seemed to be taller. As I had
suspected, one of the suits of armor must have had a
person in it, and as it moved, the girl who was with
us screamed. My girlfriend and I laughed as her
boyfriend ran a little ways back down the hallway.
Sorry, no ghost here. Not even a demonic entity,
unless you count a demonic entity of fear that was
moving with the guy down the hallway.

We also had a map with us, so with my girlfriend guiding us, we decided to go down to the dungeon. The guy who was with the girl from the cruise wasn't really sure about this, but trying to be as cool as he could be, he followed us from a distance. Now, I would've thought that in the dungeon of an old castle, there would be quite a few demonic entities. But if there were, they were sure not manifesting for us. I told my girlfriend that maybe they were aware that we were seers and didn't want to come out and play. She insisted that the only reason why they wouldn't want to come out and play was because I was there and they didn't want to be cast out of their longtime home.

So except for the guy who was with us screaming from time to time like a little girl and his girlfriend apologizing for him being such a little baby, we were not able to see much in the spirit. However, in the natural, this medieval castle was still fascinating.

We went to the war room, where all the swords, spears, shields, and armor were kept. I don't think most of them were original to the castle, but they were still quite a sight to see.

***

My girlfriend was a little disappointed. She had hoped to see manifestations of the spirit, not just ones that we could see on our own as seers. So sometime after 1:00 a.m., we decided to return to our rooms and get some sleep. When I went back into my room, the fire had almost died out, so I put a lot of wood on it with some kindling, and before I knew it, the room was warm and cozy again.

Then there was a knock on my door. My girlfriend had cleaned up and was getting ready for bed. She noticed that her fire had almost gone out. So, standing at my door, looking as cute as she could, she asked me if I could come to her room and get the fire started again.

I smiled with an ornery smile and said, "Need some help getting the fire started, do we?"

As always, she said, "Don't get any funny ideas. It's just that some of the logs are a little too big for me to put on the fire."

Of course, I went and helped her.

The next morning we got up and went to the large room where they had served us dinner the night before, for what I suppose was a medieval breakfast. Once again, we were seated at large tables, with meat, cheese, and bread, and they also put out platters of fruit. I'm sure fruit wouldn't have been there in the medieval times, but maybe.

On the bus ride home, my girlfriend thanked me for helping her with the fireplace the night before. She informed me that we would be going on another trip soon, where she knew there would be a lot more demonic activity. I thought that if we were really boyfriend and girlfriend, once in a while we would just go to dinner, or even sit at home and watch TV. I guess I should not be surprised, because to this point she was the only other seer I knew, and I'm pretty sure that was the only part of the relationship she was interested in.

Mauthausen was yet another concentration camp in Germany. I had met my girlfriend at Dachau, a rather strange and dark place to meet a friend, but let's face it—this was a strange and dark friendship as well. Being the alpha in the relationship, she announced to me that we were going to go visit the Mauthausen death camp, and if I was game, she wanted to stay there as it got dark. This camp was known to be one of the darkest places on earth, due to the fact that the prisoners who were brought there were most certainly there for one reason: to die. This death camp was well documented to have worked prisoners literally to death. Sometimes food and water were not given to them for up to a week at a time. Working in a granite quarry, using no tools, just their bare hands, they were forced to dig out the quarry where the concentration camp was to be built. SS guards would kill those who fell behind or were too worn out to work; this was the most physically brutal concentration camp in the Nazi regime.

The camp was located in Austria. The trip south, from where we lived, was always incredible; as we came to the site of the camp, once again, it was hard to believe that these atrocities had been committed in such a peaceful place. We entered the camp with a group of people and a guide to explain where we were in the camp. I had little doubt that my girlfriend had no plans of staying with the rest of the people, but my love of history seemed to prevail, and she allowed us to at least stay close enough so I could hear what the guide was saying. As we were walking, I couldn't help but think how very quiet this place was now. The screams could no longer be heard by our group of tourists walking silently through the camp. In the spirit, both my girlfriend and I could once again see piles of demonic entities, but only in the buildings. To my surprise, for the first time in quite some time, I could see faint silhouettes of light moving about the grounds, and the lower the sun became, the easier it was to make out these angelic beings. I asked my girlfriend what she was seeing outside the buildings.

She said, "Obviously you're seeing things in the spirit that I am not."

I asked her, "Do you sense a spirit of peace out here?"

She replied, "All I know is that it's very quiet. I suppose it's because the people in our tour are being respectful."

She asked our guide if it was OK if we stayed in the camp once the sun started to go down. He said that would be fine and asked if we had flashlights, due to the fact there were only a few lights in the facility. Of course, my girlfriend said no, that we would only be in the camp for a short time.

That was when we started to wander off from the rest of the group. She did not want to be outside the buildings. I think the fact that there were angelic beings out there made her uncomfortable. She would much rather be in the buildings with the darkness and the demonic entities.

Once we were back inside the buildings, she asked me to give her a minute or so. I stood in the doorway while she walked in by herself. I could hear her speaking in low tones but could not make out what she was saying.

I stepped out of the doorway, back into a grassy area. As I turned around, I could see two of these shining figures, about the same height as I, and they were about twenty feet away. I was starting to walk toward them when a voice seemed to come to me from nowhere and said, "Go back to her now. She needs you."

So I quickly walked back to the doorway and walked in. She was sitting on the ground crying. As I went over to her and put my hand on her shoulder, she said that they were saying terrible things to her. "I thought, "They're demons. What do they usually say to you?" But of course, I said nothing.

We got up and walked outside. The two shining entities were still in the same place. Without saying anything to her, I walked in their direction until I was standing directly in front of them. I gave her a hug and asked if she was OK. She said that for whatever reason, when she was with me, she felt safe.

I said, "I think what you're sensing are the angelic beings standing right next to us. I know this is a strange place to ask, but I could lead you in a prayer, and I'm pretty sure afterward you would be able to see the angels as I do."

She said, "That's the thing I like about you. Most guys would try to make a move on a girl that was trembling in their arms, but not you. Nope. You ask if I want to be led in a prayer. In some ways, I think you are stranger than me."

With that, we left the camp. She asked if I thought it would be OK if we went and got dinner and stayed the night in an Austrian inn.

I said, "OK, but no funny business."

She said, "I wouldn't think of it."

***

As always, we stayed in two rooms, and the next morning we met each other downstairs for breakfast. She asked if I would like to go see Zugspitze, a mountain range between Austria and Germany. It was about a four-hour drive. When we arrived, I was informed that we would be taking a tram up to the top of the mountain, and we would be eating lunch at the restaurant on the peak.

As always, if nothing else, I was consistently agreeable, so we were off to take a fifteen-minute tram ride to the top of Zugspitze. The views were like nothing I'd ever seen before, and I felt as if we reached the top way too quick. Once off the tram, the views were again amazing, but the wonderful restaurant up there made it even better.

After we ate lunch, at probably the highest altitude ever in my life (except for maybe on an airplane), there was a peak that you could free climb that was at about the same height as the restaurant. So my girlfriend asked me if I would climb over to the other peak so that she could get a picture of me. As she said this, another American couple was having the same conversation. So the two ladies started talking and decided that we would climb to this other peak together. After introducing ourselves, I thought, "If this guy is game to go with me, I'm in."

So that was what we did. We climbed out of a perfectly good viewing stand near the restaurant and began descending about eighty feet into this area where you could climb up onto the next peak. I was used to jumping out of airplanes, but I had also been equipped with a parachute, and this seemed a little crazy just for a picture. The guy I was with asked me if I wanted to go back. I told him that once I started doing something, then that was what I was going to do, so if he wanted to go back, I would go on by myself. He said that if he went back by himself, he would never hear the end of it, so reluctantly he followed me up this mountain.

I had no doubt that there was a demonic entity of fear somewhere near us and maybe on both of us, but I wasn't about to let that stop me. The next thing I knew, we were on top of this peak. I guess this was not a feat that was done very often, because when we arrived, everyone from the viewing platform started snapping pictures. The area we had climbed to was about the size of a coffee table. My reluctant friend was holding on to the surrounding rocks with white knuckles. Since I was rather muscular, people yelled across to me and asked me to flex my muscles. I thought, "It's not bad enough that I am perched on this rock about the size of a coffee table, but now they want me to flex for them."

So from my knees, I did my best to accommodate them, as my new climbing friend was all but lying on his stomach, holding on for dear life.

Someone from the crowd on the viewing platform yelled, "Take off your shirt, Arnold, and stand up!"

The crowd on the platform loved that idea, but there was no way in the world it was ever going to happen. Being as cool as I could, I laughed and climbed down the mountain and back to the viewing tower. People were clapping for me and patting me on the back. My girlfriend just looked at me and said, "If I hadn't made you do it, you would have never gone." She might have been right, but at that moment, I seemed to be in the spotlight, and people were offering to buy me food. She said, "Everywhere we go, people just seem to like you."

I said, "I'm pretty sure it's just the presence of God."

She said, "I have some people I may want to introduce you to. I think they may like you as well."

***

In the weeks following, I didn't really see my girlfriend at all. Maybe it was because we weren't actually boyfriend and girlfriend. She made it clear that I wasn't really her type, only that she liked hanging out with me because we had a common gift as seers. But as a general rule, she knew where to find me, and while I was in the gym lifting weights, I heard this voice behind me saying, "Hey fly boy, do you need a spot? That looks pretty heavy."

I turned and looked at her and replied, "Nope. I think I got this."

She said, "Those people that I thought you would like to meet are gathering on Saturday. Why don't you go with me?"

I said, "Well, I don't have to work, and really have nothing else planned. So sure, why not?"

***

In the natural, as my eyes came back into focus, I realized that in that moment, God had shown me where I had come from and how I had come to be at this place. No one in the fallout shelter had moved. It was as if they were frozen in time while God had brought me into this moment.

The man who seemed to be in charge in the back of the room said, "Tell me, seer, can you see? Or do you just sense the fear in this room?"

I said, "I see three guys besides you and an assortment of knives, which I realize your buddy doesn't know how to use. So unless you're going to produce an AK-47, I see nothing to fear."

Continuing, I said, "But in the spirit, I think you and I both know that you are in a world of trouble. Maybe these demonic entities that you entertain know the word of God better than you do, but I have no doubt 'that at the name of Jesus every knee shall bow, of things in heaven, and things in the earth, and things under the earth'" (Philippians 2:10).

The man in the back of the room spoke some words in German. As he did, some of the entities manifested themselves into the size of men. The man smiled proudly.

"Really!" I said. "In Jesus's name, appear to us in your true form."

They immediately shrank down into the form of medium-size chimpanzees. I was pretty sure by this point that I wasn't going to be leading anybody in this room to the Lord, but in the natural, as well as in the spirit, I felt I had by far the upper hand, and I said, "It's really not too late. We can go about this a different way."

The man in the back of the room said, "How's that?"

I said, "There's always Romans 10:9."

He smiled again, but with a little less pride, and said to my girlfriend, "You know what you need to do to make this right, don't you?"

She said, "You know I'm not going to do that."

Curious, I said, "What do you want her to do?"

He said, "Curse you! What, you thought we were going to beat you up? You're a little too big for that, and your girlfriend has already told us that with your particular military training, it probably wouldn't be a good idea to come at you in the natural."

Again he addressed my girlfriend. "You know what to do, so do it."

She stood there and said nothing.

With that, the man stood up and said, "It doesn't really matter about those bones that were thrown at your feet when you came in. You won't last long enough to tell anyone about this room or us."

The room went silent. The demonic entities seemed unsure of their place in all this, but still they clung to their hosts. Other demonic entities stared, as if waiting for instructions.

I said, "I'm a little tired of playing games with you. In Jesus's holy name, I bind you, demonic spirits, as well as the devil that sent you. You have no place in this room. With that, I cast you out in Jesus's name."

It was as if a spotlight was turned on at the top of the stairs and made its way into the room. Even with half of the candles being put out by the demonic entities, the room was incredibly bright. The demonic spirits had received their instructions, which I am sure they had known were coming. The girl who was holding my friend by the hair released her and fell to the ground, appearing to be unconscious. The guy whose hand was bleeding from the knife vomited, and before he fell in it, he caught himself on the edge of the table. He then staggered a few steps and sat on the concrete floor.

The man in the back of the room yelled, "You think you've won this thing, Christian boy, but if I were a betting man, I think we will be reading about you here real soon!"

All that I knew was that when I walked into this fallout shelter, it was filled with darkness, fear, and demonic presence, and now, if only for a few moments, it was filled with light and the presence of God.

***

My girlfriend walked over to some of the tables and did her best to flip them over. I would've helped her, but in the moment, it seemed she needed to do it herself. She walked past me and out of the room. As I glanced back in, every person in the room was either lying on the floor or sitting exhausted.

I turned back toward the door and followed my girlfriend out and into the hallway. She kicked one of the coffee-can-size candles sitting on the floor, and I realized that not one of them was still lit.

We then went up the stairs and out of the shelter.

***

I had never really seen her mad before, and I was hoping that she was mad at the people in the fallout shelter and not me. After all, she was my only ride home. It wasn't as if my new "friends" I had just left on the floor were going to give me a ride anywhere. I ran over to the fence that we had climbed under and picked it up for her. She went under the fence and just kept walking, so I held the fence myself with one hand and crawled under.

Jogging to catch up to her, I said, "I'm sorry about your friends back there."

She said, "Well, they're not my friends anymore."

For such a short person, she walked really fast when she was mad. I had to do a slow jog just to keep up. As we got to the car, and she unlocked the doors, I quickly got in the passenger seat, thankful that I was actually sitting in the car and not watching it drive away from the parking lot. As we pulled out of the parking lot and her tires squealed a little, I said a very quiet prayer under my breath.

Doing my best to calm her down, I apologized once again.

She said, "Don't apologize. This was my fault. I had no idea what was going to happen, but I thought that as well as you and I got along, they would probably give you a chance. You know, I've never seen anything like that before. I'm pretty sure that I may have just seen my first angel or something like that. Did the room down there seem to get brighter to you?"

I said, "To me, when the presence of God filled the room, it got a lot brighter in there."

She said, "You know they put some type of a curse on you, right?"

I said, "I don't really know what that means, but I doubt it will amount to much."

She said, "I'm sure that God has given you, as a Christian, some type of power over that."

I said, "You've never referred to God like that before. Are you starting to believe that my God is God? Or do you still trust the little god of this earth?"

She said, "I never said that God didn't exist; I just said I'm not ready to become a Christian yet."

I said, "Really? Not even after that?"

The rest of the ride home was fairly quiet. As she dropped me off at my dorm and drove off, one of my friends in the parking lot said, "I'm so bored. What did you do today?"

Chapter 8

In the weeks that followed my experience at the fallout shelter, my life continued along the same path it always had. I was not able to tell anyone about what had taken place in the Black Forest of West Germany, but the events would play out in my mind from time to time until it started to fade. The one and only person with whom I was able to discuss what had happened was avoiding me. People at her office said that she was out on appointments or not able to take a phone call right then, but they would give her the messages. I had always thought that at some point when she was ready, she would show up, and our strange relationship would go on as it always had. Until that time, I would just keep doing the things I had always done.

***

Since I was permanently loaned out to a security squadron, we were all on a rotation schedule for different tasks throughout the base. On this particular weekend, I was assigned to one of the gate guard posts. We would check for stickers on cars to make sure they were registered with the base, as well as for identification cards. In the eighties, many acts of terrorism took place throughout Western Europe. As a precaution, when one came onto a military installation, there were multiple checkpoints. On this particular shift, I was at the first checkpoint. We would look at identification cards and visually look into the car, as well as use mirrors to look under a vehicle before it would proceed on to the next checkpoint. This routine was repeated for your entire shift. Most of the cars that we would inspect were smaller European cars, and on occasion, we would see an American-built car, but those were few and far between. All large trucks and delivery trucks were diverted to a different gate and would be inspected thoroughly at those checkpoints.

On this specific day, I saw an older American-built four-door car in the line. They were easily spotted because they were so much larger than the European cars and quite a bit heavier. As I walked up to the car, I asked for their identification. The driver answered, but not in English or German, so I asked him again for his identification or paperwork. Again he said something to me that I didn't understand.

I radioed for backup, hoping that someone else could translate, and I continued my visual inspection inside the car. The man kept talking to me, and in my best version of European sign language, I tried to tell him to hold on for a minute.

Someone else was coming. I took out my telescopic mirror and started to look under the car.

He yelled something to me. I looked at him, confused. I could see, in my peripheral vision to my left, as I was on the driver's side, that another airman was on his way. I glanced at my mirror and looked back at him. I saw a demonic entity leaning over him from the back seat. Then another entity appeared. This one seemed to come from the floorboard on the passenger side of the car. The entities were about level with the man's waist. It caught me off guard, so I stepped back, still facing the car.

The next thing I knew, there was a loud explosion and fire. At first, as dumb as it may sound, I really didn't know what had happened. Maybe I was in shock. Evidently, a bomb had gone off under the car. It must've been near the gas tank, because fuel vapor as well as liquid fuel had ignited. It shot out of the filler neck from the gas tank and on to me. It looked as if a ball of fire that had engulfed me. The old American car was so heavy that it barely lifted off the ground. Most of the blast was contained under the car. As the driver's luck would have it, almost all of the shrapnel went through the floorboard, severely injuring him from the waist down.

Only a small fraction of the pieces found their way to me, but at that time, that was not my concern. I was on fire, and all I could think of was to get on the ground and roll. In truth, at that moment, it was as if the nerve endings in my body seemed to just turn off, as if my brain somehow knew this was too much pain to bear. I remember thinking, "Why am I not unconscious? This would be so much easier if I was just unconscious."

As it was, I stayed alert and awake. I remember hearing sirens almost in unity as the gate sirens seemed to sing along with the sirens from the ambulance that was arriving on scene. They were the only sounds loud enough for me to hear. People were looking at me and saying things, but it was as if the volume was turned down so low that I couldn't make out what they were saying. No one else sustained any injuries, other than me and the driver of the car.

To this day, I don't know whether the man in the car lived or died. I do know that there were some loud screams coming from the car, so if he survived the blast, he was in a lot of pain. Other than that, I was never told anything. I only knew that he was alive when I was loaded into my ambulance.

My clothes were burned, and I remember looking at my left hand, thinking that I couldn't tell were my clothes ended and my hand began. There was also damage to my lower legs. Something had blown out from under the car, and I remember not being able to feel my feet.

The ambulance took me to Landstuhl hospital in Germany. The paramedic with me said that I would be taken to an intensive-care burn unit. He also told me that I was lucky (I didn't feel lucky, but I was alive) that it wasn't a small European car, because the blast would not have been contained so well, and there would've been many more injuries, as well as possible fatalities (I'm pretty sure he meant me).

***

Due to my medical training that I had received before coming into the military, as well as cross training into the security forces field, much of what they were saying made sense to me. I had received mostly first- and second-degree burns, but the paramedic thought that some of the burns were third degree. They were doing their best to remove my clothes. I'm sure that I was in shock, and I still had very little feeling in the burned areas. I couldn't tell what was going on with my feet, but I knew they were pulling out pieces of metal. They would ask me questions, and I found that it was very hard to speak. When the blast took place, I must have gasped for air and inhaled some of the flame, so my lungs, tongue, and lips were damaged. I had lifted my left arm to shield my eyes from the blast, and according to the paramedic, that was where I had received the worst of my burns. Except for a piece of scrap metal they had taken out above my left eye, my eyes seemed to be just fine. I also had a piece of scrap metal that had hit me in my chin on my left side. The paramedic assured me that the doctor would do a great job stitching it up and making it look as if I had a cleft chin—maybe a little crooked to the left, but who was going to notice that?

***

Arriving at the hospital, they rolled me into the emergency room, where nurses continued the process of removing my clothes and covering me with wet gauze. A team of German doctors came in and said that they would check on me in the morning to assess my burns. The nurses informed me that I had received burns over about 30 percent of my body, most being first- and second-degree burns. They were able to put an intravenous line, or IV, into my right arm, which wasn't damaged at all. They would have to feed me and give me all liquids from there. It felt as if I had a very bad sore throat, and they covered my mouth in wet bandages, but my head from my nose up was exposed. My left arm must have shielded my nose and eyes, and my helmet had protected my head and hair.

I would doze off to sleep from time to time and wake up thinking this was all just a bad dream.

At one point during the night, I woke up and saw two figures that looked like doctors dressed in white gowns, but they were shining and had no stethoscope. They stood at the foot of my bed just to my left; they seemed to be talking between themselves in low tones, so I could not make out what they were saying. I made a noise to let them know I was awake and aware of their presence.

As they looked at me, one of them said, "Seer, you have been spared. In the years to come, you will learn how to use your gift in a much greater way, saith the Lord."

I asked, "Who is it that I am speaking to?"

They looked at each other and smiled.

They said, "We are simply messengers that have come by way of the Lord."

I asked, "Can you stay with me?"

One of the angels said, "Your Lord has never left you. What was meant for evil shall only become a mighty testimony, as has been your entire life. Now it is time to rest and heal; the curse is no more."

I said, "Hold on! This had something to do with the curse?"

They answered again, "It is time to rest and heal."

They stayed there just looking at me until I fell back to sleep. When I woke up again to the emergency room noise, it was morning.

At that time, the doctors came into my room. While the nurses started to remove bandages, they determined that the only third-degree burns that I had received were on my left wrist and forearm. They also informed me of the procedures that would be taking place for my recovery. I was to go sit in a type of solution in what looked like a water trough for cattle; this would allow them to remove any dead skin. They said that they were going to use donor skin from a pig instead of harvesting it from me. I felt like a guinea pig, but it was worth a try. They said if it didn't work, they would have to take the donor skin from my thighs.

By this time my pain receptors were coming back online, but if I stayed very still, it didn't hurt as much. But that was where the problem came in. My therapist was convinced that it was her job to torture me and make me move. The doctors had told me that my left leg was going to be just fine, but I had received quite a bit of vascular damage to my lower right leg. They said they would do everything they could to save it, but if it came down to it, they might have to amputate.

Later that day, some of the people from my military unit came to visit me. They were made to wear gowns, masks, and shoe coverings before they came in to see me. Of course, the stupid question was, "How are you feeling?"

I just looked at them and did my best to grunt, so they handed me a pen and paper, and with my one good hand I wrote, "I feel like a pig at a barbecue, but nobody ever gave me an apple to put in my mouth." Then I wrote, "Have you talked to my girlfriend?"

He replied, "Yes, but all she did was cry, and she said that it was because of her that this happened." My friend told her that there was no way that this was her fault. All she would say was, "You don't know anything, and you wouldn't understand."

I asked him to tell her that I would be fine and that I would really like it if she would come and visit. He said that he would give her the message, but as of right now, she was pretty shaken up.

***

I was moved to the burn unit, where I would meet my two roommates. Both were army, and both had been in an explosion that was caused by a carelessly thrown cigarette butt tossed into some sort of explosive materials. They blamed it on the wind, but I'm not so sure that the army believed them. One of them was to be released in the next week; the other had more severe burns on the backs of his calves and was receiving skin grafts from his thighs. They had tried using pigskin on him, but I guess his body rejected it. I was in faith that my body would accept the pigskin because I really didn't want to have to go through the pain of them taking grafts from my thighs.

My roommate could only lie on his stomach. His parents had brought him over a video-game unit that he would play on the TV over one of the other beds. I couldn't really see what he was doing, but it seemed to take his mind off the pain. I know therapy was necessary, looking back now, but between the nurses and the therapists, I was always in a great deal of pain. To pass the time, I would read my Bible and other books.

My roommate and I thought that every time somebody came into our room, whether a doctor, nurse, or therapist, there was going to be a lot of pain involved. The only question was, Who was it going to be? He and I talked about everything. Well, he talked, and I would write on a piece of paper, crumble it up into a ball, and throw it to him. If he or I missed, I would write it down again and reattempt the effort. We would talk about where we were from, what we did in the military, and places we had gone in Europe.

Obviously I had one secret that I never shared with him, and that was the fact that I could see an angel standing beside his bed. I believe it was there because of his mother's prayers. His parents sounded as if they were very active in their local church and had also done some missionary work. He had been brought up knowing God. I had no idea in the world what that felt like. His parents would come and visit, and they would pray with him and pray with me as well, but I never felt comfortable enough to tell them that the angels that accompanied them were beautiful. I got close a few times to writing it down on my tablet, but anytime I did, I would crumble it up and throw it in my trash can.

I could feel the presence of God with us in the room, but I don't remember seeing any angelic beings standing next to me at my bed. I wanted to believe that there was someone back in the States praying for me. Maybe my dad or my half brother; maybe my sisters. My roommate's parents said that as long as they were able to, they would keep me in prayer. I had no doubt in my mind that the statement was true.

***

My friends from my unit would come and visit and try to cheer me up. I would always ask them at least once while they were there the same question: "Have you seen my girlfriend, and is she OK?" They never knew what to say except that she was not talking to any of them, and they thought she had put in for orders to another base. It didn't take much time for me to realize that I needed to quit asking that question. In truth, the only reason that I missed her so much was she was the only person I could open up to about seeing in the spirit. In some ways, the pain of not talking about what I was able to see was almost as bad as the burns.

The nursing staff did their best at keeping us active, and anytime we saw them push a sterile chrome cart into the room, we knew that those skin grafts would be for one of us. The pigskin grafts were working great on me; they never had to take any grafts from my thighs. My roommate would make jokes that every time I received my skin grafts, he would crave bacon for the next day. He would say things like "You might be related to part of my breakfast."

Soon, they were able to take the bandages off my neck and mouth. In some ways, that was a good thing, but the therapist just saw it as a new and creative way to torture me. She would make me say vowels and accentuate the shape of my mouth when I did so. It would hurt my throat and tongue, and my mouth and lips would drain fluid from the blisters and usually bleed. When my therapist was there, my roommate would just make faces, as if to say, "Man that looks like it's painful!" Every time I saw my therapist, I expected to see a small group of demonic entities following her, but it was never the case. In truth, I knew she was just doing her job to help me, but it didn't change the fact that I hated saying vowels.

My hand was healing nicely. When I first came to the burn unit, the doctors had to separate the last three fingers on my left hand. Surprisingly, I had very good use of my thumb and index finger. When I first saw my left hand, little finger looked a burnt stick.

But my range of motion was starting to return. At this time, I couldn't make a fist, but I was starting to move it better. It's surprising how much pain you can endure if you really want to. It was almost easier to endure myself having procedures done than to watch my roommate have to go through it. The doctor said that my left foot was doing great, and my right lower leg and foot were actually coming along very well. I had feeling back in my feet, and had a very strong pulse as well.

***

Finally, the day came when I was able to put water in my mouth. They told me to just swish it around and spit it out in a different cup. After I had done that a few times, they asked if I wanted to try to swallow a small amount. I was pretty sure that my desire to swallow would override any pain that I would incur. The biggest problem was, it seemed that I had lost the ability, hopefully temporary, to hold water in my mouth. So most of the water would just dribble down my chin. But still, some went down my throat. Even though it burned like a hot liquid, they said it would get easier to do the more I tried. It was frustrating, because there was generally more water in the pan under my chin than there was going down my throat. If nothing else, my roommate found this very entertaining and it would create a great sense of joy in his day.

When I was first admitted into the hospital, people came to see me quite often, but the longer I was there, the visits became less and less, until there were none. My roommate's parents had left the country as well. We were just glad that we had each other and weren't sitting in a room by ourselves.

One day, a lieutenant and a couple of NCOs came by my room and said that this incident would be put into my records as a maintenance shop accident. They went over with me exactly how I was to explain it. I didn't really understand why this was a big deal, but to me, it didn't really matter how I had gotten there—only that I was there, and I wanted to heal as quickly as possible and get back to my life.

My roommate said that he and the other troop who was in his accident got in trouble for damaging military equipment. I wasn't really sure that any actual equipment had been damaged, that my roommate and the guy who was in our room weren't being referred to as equipment owned by the US government.

Whatever the case, unfortunately for my roommate, it looked as if I would be getting out of the burn unit before him. In some ways, I was glad to be getting out, but I felt terrible for leaving him there by himself. Obviously, by this time I was able to eat food—which was pretty good, by the way— and drink liquids without dribbling down my chin. My hand and arm were still bandaged, as well as most of my scars from the burns being very visible. They had sewn up a small area above my left eye and a much larger area on my chin that tailed off to the left side of my jaw. My range of motion was pretty good, but I would have to continue seeing a therapist, even after I was released. I was still forced to say vowels on command, and I had little to no sense of taste, due to damage on my tongue. The nurses in the burn unit said they liked me better when I couldn't talk. I would crumble up notes and throw them in their direction as they entered the room. Most of them just said, "Go away!"

***

I was walking around the hospital really well now, and I was happy that the doctors were no longer using the word *amputation* concerning my lower right leg. According to them, they didn't know what the bigger miracle was—that I survived the blast, or that my body never rejected the pigskin grafts, or that my lower leg seemed to grow new veins, allowing me to keep my lower leg. I was very grateful to God for sparing me and for all my body parts being intact. My roommate assured me that we would get together at some point after he was released from the hospital; I said that would be great and looked forward to the day.

When they allowed me to go back to the dorm and I could continue my life as normal, I would go back to the burn unit in Landstuhl every week until they released him.

They put me on convalescent leave and said that as soon as my doctors and therapist allowed me to, they were going to send me back to the States to spend some much-needed time at home. As soon as I could, I would try to go back to the gym and begin the process of weight training again. I had lost some weight and continued to shed skin. The skin that was grafted onto my wrist and forearm at this time was purple in color, and I had to use a metal clamp on my left hand that attached to my thumb and index finger so that I could hold the bar and weights. It was a long process, but I had come a long way, and in my spirit, I had no doubt that this too would pass.

I really don't remember how long the process took from the day of the fire to this point, but it felt like an eternity. I went to my girlfriend's office, and they verified she had gotten orders to England. My first thought was that England really wasn't that far away, but I knew that if she had gone through these extreme measures to put whatever relationship we had in the past, I probably shouldn't pursue it any longer. Once again, I had to swallow the words that I wanted to speak to someone, anyone, and as I had done so many times before, I was to stay silent again. In all honesty, I wanted to go talk to one of the base chaplains, but I was pretty sure that that would end my military career on a bad note.

In truth, I wasn't really sure that the military wanted me to stay around much longer anyway. I had been passed over for promotion once again, and now I felt like damaged merchandise. When I reported back to my squadron, they said that I was to take immediate leave to go back home to the States and spend some R&R time there.

Home; Some Things Never Change

By this time, the doctors and my therapist had signed off on me, and with a glove on my left hand, I was able to lift weights more or less normally. So I was to take a hop (that is, a military flight) from

Rhein Main Airbase in Germany to the East Coast of the United States. At that point, I had to wait for a flight to take me to either a base in the Midwest or, preferably, a base in Southern California. I would have much rather gone to my mom and stepdad's house, where I felt a lot more comfortable. To me, this was home.

But as my luck would have it, taking a hop all the way across the country to California would have been a miracle. The next day, there was to be a flight to a base in the Midwest that was a bus ride away from my dad and stepmom's house. Of course, my dad said it would be great to see me, but I really wasn't sure how I would be received by my stepmom. So I went ahead and took the flight and arrived at the base in the Midwest.

When you take military hops, you have to be in uniform, and the only luggage I had was my military duffel bag, so everyone I came in contact with had no doubt that I was military. I took a taxi from the military base to a bus station in a large Midwest city. It felt as if all eyes were on me, but no one really said anything at all. It wasn't as if I could see all these demonic entities. It was more as if I could feel the weight of their presence in the stares of some of the people around me.

When I arrived at the bus station, I went up to the counter and told them my destination. The man at the counter was nice to me and asked me where I was stationed. I told him in Germany, and he said that his dad had been in World War II and that I should be careful, because some of the people around here didn't like what that uniform stood for.

He gave me my tickets, and I put them in my duffel bag, which had a lock on it, and went and found a seat to wait for my bus to arrive. I made sure that I sat with my back against a wall, as well as in a chair on the end of a row. I put my duffel bag between my legs and sat back to wait for them to call out when my bus was ready to board.

Unfortunately for me, I dozed off to sleep. It's hard to get rest on a military flight. When I woke up, someone had put a sign on my shirt that said Baby Killer and a few other colorful metaphors. They had also spit on me while I was asleep. So I went to the bathroom and cleaned myself up.

As I finished, they called for me to board my bus, so I hustled over, took my tickets out of my duffel bag and put the lock back on before they slid my bag into the luggage area under the bus. I got on the bus and went straight to the back, where there was a long bench seat, and sat down. Luckily, at this point, the bus was not very full, so I was able to put my backpack up on the bench seat and lie down.

If you have ever been on a bus, you know how long it takes to get anywhere, because they have to stop at every single town on the way to your destination. Every time the bus would stop, I would wake up. You could get off and stretch your legs or grab a snack. Some people would get on, and some people would get off at their destination. I would always try to get back on the bus quickly, to get the back seat. Sometimes I could see faint traces of spiritual entities on the bus with some of the riders, but then I would just close my eyes and try to go back to sleep until the next stop. Finally, I arrived at my destination.

***

As I got off the bus, I saw my dad. He came over and gave me a big hug. He said to me that I looked pretty good for going through hell and back. I asked him if we had to go straight back to the house or if it would be possible for him and me to just spend some time together. He said that my stepmom was really excited to see me, and he wanted to take me home right away. In the car ride, he asked me how things were going, and I said that things have been better, but I was glad to be out of the burn unit.

He said while I was home, he wanted to go fishing once or twice and that the car that I had had when I was stationed at the base nearby was at the house.

Sure enough, as we arrived at the duplex, my car was sitting out front, just waiting for me. We pulled into the garage, and as we got out of his car, I grabbed my duffel bag and went into the downstairs of his house. I left my bag in the room and followed him up the stairs to where my stepmom was. It was a split-level duplex, so when I went upstairs, I was actually at the front door. Then up another flight of stairs, and you would be in the living room. As I looked up, I saw my stepmom, but my eyes were transfixed on the demonic entities standing by her waist, as if they were just waiting for me.

We all sat down at the dinner table. My stepmom would do her best to play nice while my dad was there. So anytime my dad would leave the room, unless he was going to the bathroom, I tried to stay with him. Something told me that it would be a bad idea if I stayed in the room with my stepmom by myself. Even though I was much older, the spirit of fear that would come on me when I was in her presence seemed to take me back to when I was a kid in California. I'm pretty sure she would've been OK with that car bomb sending me home to meet the Lord, as opposed to me sitting at her dining room table.

At this time, the only one who knew how bad the relationship was between my stepmom and me was my dad. He would do his best to pretend that everything was OK and would try to suggest things to make the mood light. My stepmother, by this time, was on so many medications that it took both of them to keep up with it. The shaking in her hands, at least when I was around, was worse, as well as her cigarette smoking to try to calm her nerves. When her sons would come over, she would act so nice to me as well. I have no doubt that they knew very little about the spiritual battle that was taking place between us.

Looking back, I should have been more forgiving toward her, even if she would not have received it. But being young and not in a church setting being taught the word of God made it hard for me to be the Christian that I needed to be. That didn't change the fact that one of the demonic entities that she was entertaining had become intertwined with her. I'm sure that it was the spirit of deception speaking to her mind and telling her that she was so very sick and would never get well. It had also deceived her into directing her hatred for my mom toward my sisters and me. Now, I wish I would have just used my authority in the name of Jesus to bind and cast out the demons.

***

My dad, half brother, and I did get the chance to go fishing. That was always a great time, and I was able to drive my car around town. I'm sure those were the highlights of my trip. But after being there less than a week, I could feel the pressure mounting on my dad from my stepmom—that she could not tolerate my being in their home any longer. In some ways, I wish my dad would have stood up to her, but I guess in his mind, he lived with her, and I was just visiting. It was too late for me to try to get out to my mom and stepdad's house in California, but I could tell that I was running out my welcome here.

It all came to a head one day when my dad was in the garage doing something at his workbench. I went upstairs, where my stepmother was sitting at the kitchen table. She asked me (with a few colorful metaphors) how soon I was going to be leaving. I told her that I would be on military leave for more than another week.

With that, this very nonphysical, nonthreatening woman stood up, and I could see the demonic entity manipulating the situation like a puppet master. She said (again with a barrage of colorful metaphors) that she wanted me out of their house, now! As she was yelling from the top of the stairs, I was at the landing, halfway to the downstairs, and my dad was listening from the garage door. He said to me that she seemed pretty mad, and I had better find someplace else to go. My stepmother stayed at the top of the stairs yelling down at my dad and me. He wasn't really mad at me. I think he was just trying to calm my stepmom down. He asked me if I could leave the house today.

I said, "Where will I go?"

He said, starting to get mad, because the yelling from upstairs was continuing, "I don't care, as long as you leave this house."

So I started to gather up my things and shove them into my duffel bag. I gave him back the keys to my car and called for a taxi. By this point, my dad and stepmom were yelling at each other, and even though it was about me, it wasn't directed at me.

By the time I had everything shoved into my duffel bag, my dad was standing at the front door on the landing. My stepmom was still at the top of the stairs. All I could hear was them cussing at each other, and I went out the door to the garage, into the driveway. I sat on the steps leading to their front door and waited for my taxi. As I did, the front door swung open, and they both came outside. My stepmother (again with the metaphors) told me to get off her property, or she was going to call the police.

I said, "As soon as the taxi gets here, I will leave."

My dad told me, "Just do what she says, and get off the property."

I stood up with my duffel bag in my hand and walked into the front yard. At that point, I could tell that my dad had given in to a demonic entity of his own. With my stepmother still yelling that she was going into the house to call the police, my dad, now determined to get me out of his yard, walked up and said the words that I really never wanted to hear.

He said, "So, do you think you can whip me?"

I said, "Dad, I just want that taxi to show up, and I'll be gone."

But I guess the old navy man had temporarily reappeared, and he shoved me backward.

I said, "Dad, you really don't want to do this."

He said, "You think you're tough? So go ahead. Take a swing at me."

I was starting to turn around and walk to the curb when he said, "Don't ever turn your back on me."

With that, I felt a shot hit me in the right kidney. I spun back around, took him to the ground, and sat on him, with my stepmom yelling (colorful metaphors), "Now you're going to jail."

About that time, a beautiful yellow taxi showed up in front of the house. I climbed off my dad, grabbed my duffel bag, opened the door to the taxi, threw my duffel bag in, and told the driver to just get me out of there.

We drove off, and instead of going to the local bus station, I told him to drive north to a larger city and that bus station. Eyeing me, he said, "I'm sure it has something to do with you sitting on that guy back there."

I said, "Yeah, something like that."

It seemed as if what followed had been planned—the taxi driver showing up before the police and the fact that as soon as we got to the bus station, a bus was leaving with space available, for exactly where I wanted to go. I was still in my civilian clothes, so that might have helped me gain favor from the people I came in contact with. Or maybe it was just God paving a path before me.

***

I arrived at the military base and changed into my uniform so that I would be able to catch a military flight back to the East Coast. Again, my luck would continue, and by that evening, I was on a military flight heading east. While on the East Coast, I called my mom in California. I just wanted to hear a friendly voice. I told her what had happened, and she said that she was sorry that things had gone so badly at my dad's house and that she wished I would have come to California instead.

Before I knew it, I was back in Germany. My roommate asked why I was back from convalescent leave a week early. All I could say was I should have just stayed there in country and actually gotten some rest.

Kelly J Caselman

Chapter 9

When I finally went back to work with my unit, they put me in a mundane job until I could get back to 100 percent. I hated it! I had been in the weight room for quite some time by now; I had even worked out the whole time that I was at my dad's house in a local gym. Soon, I was back in football practice and trying to get my life back as normal as possible, but in my workplace, they treated me as if I were somehow different, as if maybe I were dealing with some type of psychological problem. It started to make me angry that they didn't treat me the way they used to, as if I were somehow still broken.

The doctors would ask me things such as "How does that make you feel?"

What I really wanted to say to these doctors was "The people you have coming into your office really just need the demons cast out of them." But if there was one thing I knew that I was good at, it was that I could keep my thoughts to myself, for the most part, and silence seemed to be my best option, unless I wanted to be discharged from the military on a psych evaluation.

I'm sure that there are many people in psychiatric hospitals because of their ability to see in the spirit and not stay quiet about it; I had no intentions of ever being one of those unfortunate souls. In football and in the dorm, things went back as they had been before. To my friends, I was to a degree indestructible. They would say things like "That boy has been baptized by the Holy Spirit in water and baptized by fire as well."

I think the hardest part was losing the only person I could talk to about seeing in the spirit. It was never about her being my girlfriend; she had made it perfectly clear on several accounts that she was not. It was more that I had to keep things bottled up inside, as I had for most of my life. I thought many times about my associate pastor friend in California, and I had even thought about going to England for a surprise visit to my friend, but I never did.

***

My dad would write to me a few times a month, and he apologized over and over for how he had acted when I left his house when I was on convalescent leave. I guess it was always easy to forgive him, because I wanted that relationship to be restored to what it had been before he and my mom were divorced. After all, he was my best friend growing up. We did most everything together, but I never told him about seeing in the spirit, because I had no doubt he would think that I had mental problems, as most everyone else did.

In the letters that we would send back and forth, we talked about possibly starting a key shop business back in the Midwest, where he and my stepmom lived. We thought that we could also work with safes and home and business security systems. He assured me that my stepmom was on board with this business arrangement, but he had no money, so in the beginning, I would have to be the financial backbone to the business. Really, the only money I had spent in the military overseas was on trips to other countries and camera equipment, so I actually had quite a bit of money saved up in the bank. After all, saving money had always been something I was pretty good at; when I was a kid, my sisters always knew that I had money. It was as if God had always financially provided for me, even when I was all by myself living in the janitor's closet. Jehovah Jireh is my provider.

Coming Full Circle

One weekend, some of my friends from our football team decided to take me to the Oktoberfest. They were very determined to find me a beer that I liked. I honestly do not like the taste of beer, but I was willing to taste what Germany had to offer and see if I could find anything I liked. At Oktoberfest, they had literally hundreds of varieties of beer. There were large buildings that they called beer tents and smaller tents that they called booths. They would give you small sample cups of different types of beer that the particular vendor sold; if you liked one, they would sell you a one-liter beer stein of that particular beer. Some of the women in the large beer tents could carry up to five one-liter beer steins full of beer in one hand. It was quite impressive, and also scary that these German women were that strong.

In the daytime, spiritually speaking, I didn't see a lot of demonic or angelic activity. It was just a fun event with parades and lots of people. But as the daytime started to turn to night, the spiritual activity started to change as well. The football teammates I had come with had obviously been drinking beer since we arrived. We had also eaten a lot of wonderful food, which I'm sure was the only reason they were still standing up by this time. We decided to sit and watch some of the shows, which were generally traditional German music and dancing. Of course, some of our friends, who maybe had one too many beers, decided that they would get up and dance as well. It was my job to convince them otherwise and do my best to get them to sit down.

Unfortunately, there was also an Australian rugby team in the crowd, and after the show, they came over to us and asked if we were a rugby team as well. We told them no, that we were an American-style football team and that we were stationed at a nearby military installation. In the spirit, and in the natural, I had a good idea that my guys might say something stupid, but I was wrong. It was the Australian rugby team that made the first comment, something about American football players not being nearly as tough without their padding and helmets. I am sure that if we were thinking logically, their statement had a little truth to it, but we were not about to admit that.

Now, in the supernatural realm, I could pretty much see what was about to take place, as well as the individuals who were about to make it happen. There were a lot of words going back and forth, and to be honest, a lot of what they were saying to us we really didn't understand, and I wasn't even drunk.

The Australian rugby team started to huddle up and push us backward. We didn't really understand what they were doing, or why, so we attempted to push back, with very little effectiveness. The next thing we knew, some German policeman came in and, speaking German, told us to break it up. I spoke back to them in German and told them they were going to have to help me separate the two groups.

After that, they warned the Australians, as well as my guys, that if anything else like this happened, we would be removed from the premises.

The Australians were entertained by the whole event. My football buddies were a little bit angrier and wanted to prove that they were as tough as the Australians. Luckily, I was able to convince them that there was a lot more food to eat, beer to drink, and girls to be turned down by. With that, we went on our way to eat some more food.

Surprisingly, as we were sitting at our table, some of the Australian rugby team came over and, in their own way, apologized for the incident and said they were just trying to have fun with us. They ended up sitting at the table, and we bought them all a round of beer, very much to their delight.

* * *

As the night went on, the demonic entities, as they often do, became more numerous. The guys weren't too worried about getting drunk, because we had booked a nearby hotel and had already planned on taking a taxi there. This felt familiar, as I had often felt like a babysitter when I was a kid at my sister's parties. I also knew that in this case, my size wasn't really a benefit, due to the fact that people who have had a little too much to drink seem to think they are indestructible. This made my job of keeping them out of trouble more difficult, and if that weren't enough, they were convinced there were going to be girls going back to the hotel with us. There is nothing more attractive than a staggering guy who can barely stand up.

But it was getting late, and at our table, a couple of the guys had put their heads down and were now asleep, so I convinced them that it would probably be a good time to go back to the hotel. With that, we woke up our buddies and started making our way to the area where the taxis were lined up.

While we were waiting on some benches for a taxi van, I noticed a nearby building that had an unusual amount of demonic activity. As the taxi van pulled up, we realized that all but two of us would fit in the van, so making sure that some of the soberer guys went with them, I told them I would stay behind. I wanted to go look at this building. One of my buddies who was still sober said he would stay behind with me, and we would grab a taxi together. So the majority of my friends from the football team left for the hotel.

I told my buddy that I wanted to go check out this building.

He said, "OK, but why?"

I said, "Let's just say I'm interested in what might be going on inside."

He said, "Let's go check out the building."

The building was two stories tall and had some dim lights shining from the upstairs windows, possibly candlelight. As we approached the building, the demonic entities that were around the door seemed to move away as I spoke my authority in Jesus's name under my breath.

My buddy asked, "Should we be going in here? This place is giving me the creeps."

I said, "I'm not scared; are you?"

As I walked in the door with my friend close behind, something felt strangely familiar. Maybe it was the graffiti on the walls, or maybe it was just that I was sensing a particular presence. Either way, Psalm 91 came to mind, and I began praying it under my breath over my friend and me.

We came to some stairs, and as I looked up, I saw more demonic entities sparsely placed along the stairs.

I looked at my friend and said, "This may get a little weird, so just stay with me."

He said, "OK. Well, if it's going to get weirder than this, can I wait outside?"

I said, "That's fine, but wait for me to come out."

He said, "I just hope you do come out."

With my friend still standing behind me, I looked up the stairs, and among the demonic beings was a familiar face. The guy in charge from the fallout shelter in the Black Forest looked down at me and said, "Aren't you supposed to be dead?"

My friend, as he was running back down the hallway, said, "Let's get out of here!"

I looked back up the stairs, and the demonic entity that was standing with him manifested into a Hollywood version of a demon, somewhat hulking in size. It was then that I noticed there were, what looked like, transparent angel wings wrapped around me all the way to the floor and well over my head.

Seeing that, I simply said, "In Jesus's name, I bind all your demons and the demonic entity that stands with you and say in Jesus's name, show yourself as you truly are."

With that, this Hollywood demon shrank down to the size of a medium dog.

The man from the fallout bunker slowly clapped his hands and said, "Well played, seer. You sure know how to ruin a party." He looked back into the room that he had come from and said, "It looks like all the demons up here have returned to their original size and shape, and for some reason my followers seem to be asleep or passed out."

I said, "My guess is that they didn't want your people, who have been deceived, to see them in their true form. Better to be passed out than to see who and what they are actually being deceived by. You demonic entities need to depart from this building and these premises. In Jesus's name, be gone."

The man looked at me and said, "Do you know how much I truly hate you?"

I said, "Do you want to fix that, or do you just want to continue your life serving a defeated god?"

With a smile, he said, "Where did your girlfriend go? I haven't seen her in quite some time. Is she well?"

I said, "I don't really know why you're changing the subject to her, but to answer your question, I haven't seen her since that day at the fallout shelter." It seemed so strange, because all of a sudden, he was having what seemed like a normal conversation between two people. So I asked him, "I know you see in the spirit. Do you see this angel that is standing with me?"

He said, "I see you glowing in what seems to be a goldish light, the same way you did at the fallout shelter. Is that just you shining like that, or is it your angel?"

I said, "I don't know if it's my angel, but you would be correct in saying it is the presence of an angel sent by God."

He asked, "Are you an angel, or is one just standing with you?"

I said, "I am just a man, as are you; the difference is that the Lord my God stands with me,

while your god departs in the presence of the most
high."

***

He went back into the room where he had come
from. When he came out, there were two women
with him, and they started down the stairs. They
were quite wobbly, with one hand holding on to him
and the other hand holding on to the railing. They
made their way to the bottom of the stairs where I
was standing. He seemed to be completely in his
right mind. The women with him, on the other hand,
could talk a bit, in a shaky voice, but they were still
having a little trouble walking. The man said to one
of the women, "Do you remember this guy from the
fallout shelter?"

She said, "Yes. He was the one you put the
curse on. Wasn't he supposed to die?"

The man said, "That's true. He was
supposed to die, but even when we were back at the
fallout shelter, I had my doubts that it would work
on him, because some people play by different
rules."

As they walked down the hallway and I
followed, I asked him if it was just the three of them
up there. It felt as if there were more.

The man laughed and said, "There are more
of my people up there, but when the demons started

screaming and moving about the room, I assumed there was a reason, so I went to the door and looked down the stairway. You caught me off guard. In fact, you were the last person I expected to see." He stopped by the front door of the building and said, "By the way, I don't know your name. Should I just call you the seer?"

I smiled and said, "For now, the seer will do just fine."

As we walked down the sidewalk from the building, he said, "Is that the guy you came with over there?"

I said, "Yes."

He said, "You may want to get rid of that spirit of fear that is on him."

I said, "I think I can handle that."

He said, "I have no doubt that you can." The three of them turned and went down the street.

As I approached my friend waiting for me on the curb across the street, he said, "What did you do in there? It sounded like you were throwing tables and chairs, and I was waiting for someone to come flying out of the second-story window. Who was that the man from the top of the stairs that didn't seem to like you?"

I said, "Are you ready to grab a taxi and head for the hotel?"

He said, "In truth, I went over to the phone booth and called for a taxi, and it's on the way now." He asked me, "So, what was all that noise I heard?"

I said, "I really don't know. I actually never made it past the bottom of the stairs where you left me."

He said, "I don't believe that at all, because I heard things being thrown around and loud crashes. I don't know what actually happened in there, but I think you must have won the fight, because you don't seem to have one scratch on you."

I said, "Sometimes you don't have to physically fight at all to win. Sometimes you just show up, and God fights for you."

Just then, a taxi pulled up. I said, "Let me tell you about a verse in the Bible—2 Kings 6:12–17—about a man named Elisha."

**

Some months later, in the winter of 1986, I was walking through the woods on a dirt path that I had walked hundreds of times; it was a path that led from my air force dorm down to the military fitness center that I had worked out at for years. The path that I was walking on would usually take me about twenty minutes to walk. The forest was thick with trees, and as I was walking, I noticed an angelic entity walking next to me. I asked as we walked, "Are you a messenger or just walking with me?"

The angel just smiled and kept walking.

I said, "You do know that I'm going to the fitness center to work out. Are you going to follow me all the way there?"

All he said was "Yes, I know where we are going."

As we arrived at the gym, there was no attendant seated at the window; just a clipboard for me to sign in. And there were no other names on the clipboard. I was the first.

So I yelled in the window and said, "So, I guess I'm supposed to just sign in and go on back."

There was no answer. I looked at the angel standing next to me and said, "That's weird." So I signed in and went on back to the weight room area.

Once again, as I started gathering weights, I noticed that I was also the only one in the weight room. I looked at the angel and said, "Do you know what's going on?"

He just smiled, so I began my workout. And as I did, the angel began to speak to me.

He said, "This is a place that, in the future, I will come to speak to you often—in your weight room, and by yourself. Because it is in this place that you are the most focused, and your mind is not as cluttered with day-to-day concerns."

I said, "I know this is not why you're here, but where is everyone?"

He said, "They will come soon enough. I have been given a message to relay to you. Some of the messages I will speak to you in the future are not for you to remember but are given to you to pass on to others. You will have very little memory of these messages. But some of the messages are for you to hear and to remember. This is one of those messages you are to remember.

"To this point, there have been three attempts to take your life: The lightning bolt was meant to claim three lives and not just one that day. The gunman at the fast-food restaurant where you worked was supposed to kill you and some of your coworkers. And also, more recently, the car bomb was meant to take your life as well as others. The accuser has had three attempts to remove you from the path that is before you, and by the name of the Lord thy God, he has failed.

"He will try again, and again he will fail. The prayers you have prayed over yourself for many years have set a hedge of protection securely around you. It was not by an accident that you came upon these words as a child, but it was by God's hand that you learn to speak the words into existence. This hedge of protection will sometimes appear to you, the seer, as angel's wings that seem to completely cover you at times.

"Trust in the Lord your God, and he will open many doors before you. Know the Lord your God and his voice, for the deceiver will attempt to change the path that God has set before you. You have just started your journey. The Lord has sent ministering spirits to go before you and prepare your way. You will be taken to a dry place, a desert, and it is there that you will be given instructions. You will be taught the word of God, and you will grow, and things will come to you that cannot be easily explained. Temptation will come and try to move you away from this path. But always trust in the Lord thy God, and keep your feet steadfast on the rock, for you have just begun this path. Remember, seer, the testimony that is before you is greater than what you have experienced in the latter, but that testimony is yet to be told. Soon you will tell that testimony as well."

About the Author

Kelly is an ordained minister, small business owner and United States military veteran. His desire is for people to understand the gifts of the spirit and how they apply to everyday life. Seeing into the supernatural is a much misunderstood gift and for those that have it can be scary and isolating. He wants people to know that they are not alone and ultimately learn their authority in Christ. Kelly makes his home in the high desert of eastern New Mexico with his wife, three grown children and grandchildren.

Kelly J Caselman